WITH MANCHESTERS IN
THE EAST

The Battalion Officers on Mobilization, August 1914

[*Photo: Warwick Brookes*]

Front Row, left to right—Rev. E. T. Kerby, Chaplain; Capt. C. Norbury; Capt. H. G. Davies; Capt. and Adj. P. H. Creagh; Major G. B. Hurst; Lieut.-Col. H. E. Gresham; Major J. H. Staveacre; Major J. Scott; Capt. J. N. Brown; Capt. H. Smedley.

Middle Row, left to right—————; Lieut. F. Hayes; Capt. J. F. Farrow (R.A.M.C.); Lieut. G. Chadwick; Lieut. W. G. Freemantle; Lieut. C. H. Williamson; Capt. A. T. Ward Jones; Lieut. W. F. Creery; Capt. C. E. Higham.

Back Row, left to right—Capt. T. W. Savatard; Lieut. B. Norbury; Capt. D. Nelson; Lieut. D. Norbury; Lieut. E. Townson; Lieut. G. S. Lockwood; Lieut. J. H. Thorpe; Lieut. G. C. Hans Hamilton; Lieut. H. D. Thewlis; Lieut. A. H. Tinker.

Absent—Capt. R. V. Rylands.

WITH MANCHESTERS IN THE EAST

BY

GERALD B. HURST

The Naval & Military Press Ltd

Reproduced by kind permission of the Central Library,
Royal Military Academy, Sandhurst

Published by
The Naval & Military Press Ltd
Unit 10 Ridgewood Industrial Park,
Uckfield, East Sussex,
TN22 5QE England
Tel: +44 (0) 1825 749494
Fax: +44 (0) 1825 765701
www.naval-military-press.com
www.military-genealogy.com
www.militarymaproom.com

In reprinting in facsimile from the original, any imperfections are inevitably reproduced and the quality may fall short of modern type and cartographic standards.

PUBLISHERS' NOTE

DURING the passage of this book through the press, the Author has been engaged overseas on active service, and has been unable to devote the necessary attention to the correction of the proofs, etc. Due allowance must therefore be made for such errors as have crept into the pages.

The Publishers have felt obliged to delete the numbers of the Territorial Battalions mentioned in the book, a fact which accounts for occasional vagueness in terminology.

CONTENTS

	PAGE
PUBLISHERS' NOTE	v

CHAPTER		
I.	EASTWARD HO!	1
II.	THE SUDAN	12
III.	GALLIPOLI	23
IV.	THE AUGUST BATTLES AT CAPE HELLES	33
V.	TRENCH WARFARE ON GALLIPOLI	45
VI.	THE STRAIN	56
VII.	THE LIMIT	65
VIII.	LAST WORDS ON GALLIPOLI	71
IX.	REVIVAL IN EGYPT	76
X.	ON THE SUEZ CANAL	82
XI.	SINAI	88
XII.	THE TERRITORIAL IDEA	95
	APPENDIX—EXTRACT FROM A LETTER FROM GENERAL WINGATE	100
	INDEX	103

LIST OF ILLUSTRATIONS

The Battalion Officers on Mobilization, August 1914	*Frontispiece*
	FACING PAGE
Lieut.-Col. H. E. Gresham	2
Arrival at Khartum, 2nd October 1914	10
General Sir F. R. Wingate, G.C.B., K.C.M.G.	14
Map of Gallipoli	24
(*a*) In Khartum Station (*b*) In a Turkish Trench	40
C Company, The British Camel Company	62
Group of Officers, Egypt, 1914	84

With Manchesters in the East

CHAPTER I

EASTWARD HO!

OUR Battalion of the Manchesters was typical of the old Territorial Force, whose memory has already faded in the glory of the greater Army created during the War, but whose services in the period between the retreat from Mons and the coming into action of "Kitchener's Men" claim national gratitude.

Their earlier history hardly emerges from parochialism. Founded in 1859 and recruited mainly from the southerly suburbs of Manchester, the Battalion lived through the common vicissitudes of the English Volunteer unit. It knew the ridicule and disparagement of the hypercritical and cosmopolitan, the too easy praise of the hurried inspecting general, the enthusiasm of the camp fire, the chill of the wet afternoon on a wintry rifle range at Crowden. The South African War gave many a chance of active service, and infused more serious and systematic training in the routine of the yearly Whitsuntide camps. At that time everything depended on the Regular officer who acted as adjutant, and officers and men owed much to the inspiring energy of Captain (now Colonel) W. P. E. Newbigging, C.M.G., D.S.O., of the Manchesters, whose adjutancy (1902-1907) meant a great step in their efficiency. The letter " Q," which signifies success in all examinations required by the War Office, figured in the Army List after most of our officers' names during this vivid and strenuous phase. For the rest, the pre-War period turned mainly on the fortnightly camps and occasional Regimental exercises. Salisbury Plain, the Isle of Man, Aldershot and a few North Country areas are full of memories of manœuvre and recreation in a peaceful age. Regimental exercises filled weekends in Cheshire or the West Riding.

Volunteering served many purposes in England. It kept alive in luxurious times a sense of discipline and a cultivation of endurance. Its comradeship brought classes together so closely that the easy relationship between officers and men in the 1st line Territorial unit of 1914-1915 was the despair of the more crusted Regular martinet. Its joyous amateurism freed it from every trace of the mental servitude which is the curse of militarism, and stimulated initiative and individuality. Long before the War, most Territorials believed in universal training, not so much on account of the German peril, which to too many Englishmen seemed a mere delusion, as on account of its social

Jerome, Southport.

Lieutenant-Colonel H. E. GRESHAM.

value. It is pleasant to remember how solidly Lord Roberts received local Territorial support when he made the most prophetic of all his speeches in the Free Trade Hall, Manchester, on the 22nd October 1912.

Lord Haldane's conversion of the Volunteers into the Territorial Force of 1907 meant little change in the internal economy or in the personnel of this Battalion. Its mounted infantry company, 140 strong, and its cyclists were lost in the interest of uniformity. Nevertheless, the change made us better fitted for war by incorporating us in the larger Divisional organisation essential in European war. Volunteer units supplied select companies for South Africa in 1899 and 1900. The East Lancashire Territorial Division was ready to take the field *en bloc* against the Germans in 1914.

The story to be told in these pages is so largely that of one battalion that a word can be said of its leaders in August, 1914, without making any claim to special pre-eminence, for our old and honourable rivalries with other local battalions faded long ago in mutual confidence.

Lieutenant-Colonel H. E. Gresham, who had commanded since 1912, was an ideal C.O.—a Territorial of long service and sound judgment, a fine shot, and in civil life a distinguished engineer. In Major J. H. Staveacre, the junior Major, we had an incomparable enthusiast, with a zest for every kind of sport, a happy gift of managing men and an almost professional aptitude for arms which had been enriched by his experiences in the Boer War. Captain P. H. Creagh of the Leicestershire Regiment was a fine adjutant, whose ability and character were to win him recognition in wider fields. His management of our mobilisation was beyond praise. The quartermaster, Major James Scott, was an old Manchester Regiment man, with a record of good work at Ladysmith and Elandslaagte. Of the company officers and N.C.O.'s, there is no need to add here to the tribute which will be theirs in any detailed history of Gallipoli. Nothing was more characteristic than their readiness to volunteer for foreign service as soon as we mobilised—long before the immensity of the War was understood, and considerably before the day of the lurid poster and the recruiting meeting.

The Manchester Territorial Infantry Brigade was embodied on the 4th August 1914, and on the 20th marched out through Rochdale to a camp on the Littleborough moors near Hollingworth Lake, where they were asked to offer themselves for service abroad. Twenty-six officers and 808 men of our Battalion (roughly, 90 per cent. of our strength) volunteered. A wise pledge, afterwards unavoidably broken, was given by the authorities that no man should be transferred from his own unit against his will.

We dropped down the Channel on the evening of the 10th September 1914 in a convoy of fourteen transports and one ammunition ship, with H.M.S. *Minerva* as escort—the first Territorial Division that ever left England on active service. We sailed in a ship with a few East Lancashire details and the Headquarters Staff of the Brigade. General Noel Lee, the Brigadier, was an old Manchester Territorial officer, who understood the Territorial spirit to a nicety, and his death from wounds received in the battle of the 4th June 1915 was our irreparable loss. The Brigade Major was a tower of strength when on Gallipoli.

Of our Battalion, who enjoyed during those shining autumn days their first vision of Gibraltar "grand and grey," with its covey of German prizes in harbour, and of the Mediterranean, then free of the submarine, and who half feared that the War would be over while they were still buried in the African desert, only a small number survive unscathed. Many sleep amid the cliffs and nullahs of Gallipoli.

The virtues and capacities of these my comrades will always haunt my imagination. Their psychology was extraordinarily interesting. They were unlike the Regulars, who preceded them in the field, and to some extent unlike the New Army, which gathered in their wake.

They had very little of the professional soldier. Only 45 among them had ever served in the Regular Army. Their homes and callings and the light amusements of a great city filled their minds in the same way as the Regimental tradition and routine filled those of the old British Regular Army. With a few exceptions, the feeling of duty was a far stronger motive to their soldiering than any love of adventure. These Manchester men had little of the Crusader or Elizabethan but his valour. They were, in fact, almost arrogantly civilian, coming from a country which had dared ineptly to look down on its defenders. The Northerner is not an enthusiast by nature. His politics are usually limited to concrete questions of work and wages, prices and tariffs, and he knows no history. The Germans in August, 1914, were still " Lancashire's best customers "—not a warlike race bent on winning world-empire by blood and iron. The social traditions of the middle-class urban population, from which the Territorials were drawn, had never fostered the military spirit, nor the power to recognise and understand that spirit in others. In such circumstances the sober zeal with which middle-aged sergeants forsook their families and businesses at the very outset of the War, without a moment's hesitation, is a signal proof of their character. No men were ever greater lovers of peace. Some philosophers have seen or tried to see in the War a judgment on the luxury and frivolity of pre-War England, on her neglect of defence, and her absorption in opulence. Were this the case, it would be ironical to reflect how the North Country homes, first and most cruelly scourged by the War, were homes to which the so-called " sins of society " were least known and most repugnant, and where military training had been long pursued in the teeth of public ridicule and at the sacrifice of leisure. Long afterwards the father of a very talented private (Arthur Powell), who was killed in Turkey, wrote of his son : " We never intended him for the rude alarums of war, but his sense of duty and the horrors of Belgium fired his imagination, so that with hundreds of thousands of high-spirited young Englishmen, he placed himself in his country's service." This cast of thought is uncommon in the ranks of a Regular army.

Officers and N.C.O.'s were obviously and admittedly amateurs, and never acquired the distinctive dash of the old Army. Soldiering was not their profession. Yet Territorials like the Manchesters possessed a range of talent in many ways beyond the normal standard of the Army. They had the manual arts and crafts of the industrial North. These volunteers were in civil life builders and joiners ; railwaymen, tramway-men, engineers ; clerks, shorthand - writers, draughtsmen, warehousemen, packers ; carters and fitters ; telephonists, chemists. When half of C Company was suddenly converted into the British Camel Corps at Khartum it was discovered to contain the camel-keeper of Bostock's menagerie. We found piano-tuners for the Sirdar's Palace, gardeners for the Barrack plantations, and in later days expert mechanics for anti-aircraft gunnery. Skilled clerks like Sergeants J. C. Jones and Beaumont were marked out by Nature for the orderly room. Many men well qualified to hold commissions served in the ranks and died before the nation recognised their quality. Lastly, we could turn out more barristers than all the other East Lancashire units put together. It would be hard to imagine better officers than our three ex-Juniors of the Northern Circuit— N. H. P. Whitley, J. H. Thorpe and Hans Hamilton.

With the New Army, that was destined to do so much to save the cause of civilisation, our men had more in common than with the Regulars. In 1914, however, we had inevitably a less thorough training in technique than that which fell to their lot in the ensuing years. Only a few of our officers had gone the round of "schools of instruction" and "courses." We had fewer specialists, and our equipment was probably inferior. During all our Eastern experiences we used the long rifle only. It was, however, a real advantage to have had nearly sixty years' record as a Volunteer unit behind us, with all sorts of Regimental traditions, which lie at the roots of comradeship and ensure happy relations between officers and men. Another distinctive virtue of the Territorial system about Manchester was that all ranks, from Brigadier-General to private, came from one neighbourhood, and viewed life from much the same angle. They ran to type, and their interest in soldiering, obviously spontaneous in the first instance, had been fostered by common experiences in time of peace.

We saw Malta in the far distance on the evening of the 21st September, and next day, in mid-afternoon, our convoy unexpectedly met an Indian Division on its way from Bombay to Marseilles. Their transports, mainly British

Indian liners, passed ours and exchanged escorts with us, thrilling the least imaginative with pride in the Empire and a sense of the illimitable issues at stake in Europe. We had left England ringing with the legendary passage of the Russians from Archangel, the snow still clinging to their furs, just as the British Army in Spain, in 1812, had been cheered by a similar mirage of Russians streaming to their aid through Corunna. The first paper that we read on reaching Egypt announced in giant headlines the arrival of 250,000 no less shadowy Japanese at Antwerp. But the Indians were real. Their appearance was a true touch of the World War and they reached the firing line in Flanders on the 19th October.

We eventually arrived at Alexandria on the 25th September 1914. B Company, under Captain (afterwards Lieutenant-Colonel) J. N. Brown, was dropped here, half of it under Captain E. Townson going on to Cyprus, which they garrisoned until the eve of its annexation. Eventually the whole Company, then under Captain (afterwards Major) D. Nelson, was reunited to the rest of the Battalion when it left for the Dardanelles. The remaining part of the Division also disembarked at Alexandria, in order to relieve the Regular garrisons of Alexandria and Cairo. The Battalion passed on to Port Said. As we neared the harbour, our men hailed watchers on the quay for the latest news. Antwerp was then at its last gasp, and the *Aboukir*, *Hague* and *Cressy* had been torpedoed in the

North Sea. The first cry from the ship was "How is City getting on?" League football was still the first interest of Young England in the second month of the Great War.

We sailed down the Canal on a scorching Sunday morning to Suez and the Red Sea. A few Indians guarded its banks. Onward through the misty heat, under escort of a destroyer, with a wind blowing hot from Arabia, to Port Sudan, where we put in at 11 A.M. on the 30th September. The temperature was 105° F. in the shade. Here half of C Company, under Captain T. W. Savatard (afterward skilled on Gallipoli) were left to garrison and construct defences for the place. Once a desolate coral reef, it is now a great harbour with the promise of a greater future. This first night of Africa we rowed happily across its starlit lagoon in the full glamour of the East to enjoy British hospitality.

Next morning we started, with Major Boyle of the Egyptian Army Staff as a " cicerone," on the long railway track from the sea to Atbara and Khartum, past scattered villages peopled by staring Fuzzy Wuzzies with erect and luxuriant black hair, and across hot stretches of desert and rock. At a quarter past eleven on the morning of the 2nd October 1914 we arrived at Khartum North, where we detrained and were met by the Sirdar, General Sir Reginald Wingate, then Governor-General of the Sudan, and his Staff. We marched over the Blue Nile Bridge to the spacious British barracks, the only

ARRIVAL AT KHARTUM, 2nd OCTOBER 1914.

spot in the Sudan where the Union Jack flies unaccompanied by the flag of Egypt, and relieved the Suffolk Regiment. In the afternoon our band played them out of the cantonment, and we cheered them on the first stage of their long journey to the blood-stained battle-fields of Flanders.

CHAPTER II

THE SUDAN

THE tasks allotted to the Battalion between October, 1914, and April, 1915, while garrisoning the Sudan were of great variety. With the gunners at Khartum Fort, they constituted part of the British force then in the country, of which Colonel Gresham was commander. The detachment left at Port Sudan organised its defences, ran an armoured train, and patrolled the Red Sea in the *Enterprise*. One group, under Captain R. V. Rylands (afterwards killed on Gallipoli), guarded the railway works at Atbara. Another under Captain B. Norbury occupied the hill station of Sinkat. Important censorship work at Wadi Halfa was entrusted to Captain J. H. Thorpe, and, when he was invalided, to Lieutenant L. Dudley, who fell later in action on Gallipoli. At Khartum a half company, under Captain C. Norbury, was on arrival transformed immediately into the British Camel Corps.

For some little time after our coming the normal social and sporting life of the small British colony at Khartum was hardly ruffled by the storm raging in Europe, and we gratefully enjoyed its warm-hearted hospitality. At the beginning of

November war broke out between Great Britain and Turkey, and the loyalty of the Sudanese was put to the test. The Germans built upon the probability of a Jihad or Holy War, and never dreamed that the handful of young Englishmen who administered the country under the Sirdar's guidance could have won its loyalty against all comers. When the Sirdar announced in English and Arabic the news of the Porte's entry into the War one shining Sunday morning in early November, to a large gathering of Egyptian and Sudanese officers and dignitaries at the Palace, their zealous unanimity was impressive. Hundreds of native notables contributed generously to British Red Cross funds. Sheikhs of the Red Sea Province, who had once been dervish partisans, showed me with glowing pride when at Port Sudan silver medallions with King George's likeness, given by him to them on his visit to Sinkat.

Few pages of history are more wonderful than that which records the conversion of the chaotic and down-trodden Sudan of 1898 into the peaceful and prosperous Sudan of to-day. Scepticism as to the uses of Empire, which too often beset the Manchester man at home before the War, was dissipated by seeing what Anglo-Egyptian sovereignty and British character and industry have achieved in a land so long tormented by slave-traders and despots. The happy black boys of Gordon College go to school with books under their arms, and play football, coached by Old Blues and cheered by enthusiastic comrades.

On the 30th October (Kurban Bairam day) the Manchesters saw the Sirdar bestow gaily coloured robes of honour on deserving chiefs. Everywhere were signs of economic progress. The cotton-growing plantations on the Gezira Plain, the ginning factory at Wad Medani, the numerous irrigation and public health works, the research laboratories of Gordon College, the industries of Khartum North and of Atbara, all bore the distinctive hall-mark of British Imperialism.

The magic of the British name in the Sudan seemed to us to rest not only on the art of government but on the great memories of Gordon and Kitchener and the abiding influence of General Wingate's personality. The Gordon statue at Khartum is almost a shrine. The Sudan itself is Lord Kitchener's monument. During our life there we were daily witnesses of General Wingate's tact, power and example. In all Mohammedan areas of the Sudan, Great Britain is wisely defender of the faith, and Islam is wisely with Britain. On the 19th November we were entertained at the Egyptian Army Officers' Club on the occasion of the Mohammedan New Year. On the 27th January 1915 the Prophet's birthday was celebrated with rapturous pageantry, and the Sirdar and Lady Wingate paid most impressive visits to the pavilions set up by the principal sheikhs and notables in front of the mosques at Khartum and Omdurman, while huge crowds of religious enthusiasts beat tom-toms and sang outside. We saw the Sirdar reviewing his

[Elliot & Fry Ltd.

General Sir F. R. WINGATE, G.C.B., G.C.V.O., K.C.M.G., G.B.E., D.S.O.
Honorary Colonel of the Battalion.

Egyptian and Sudanese troops at Khartum, formally inspecting the schools, hospitals, barracks and prisons around Port Sudan, decorating veterans with medals, and addressing in every native dialect the political and religious leaders of the people. We found that no men appreciated the care and skill of the Red Sea Province hospital more warmly than Arabs from the then Turkish territory of Jiddah.

The whole history of the evolution of the Sudan is epitomised in the bare, sun-scorched Christian graveyard of Wadi Halfa. The sandy, high-walled enclosure is the common resting-place of four successive generations of British Empire builders : first, of soldiers who fell in the Gordon Relief Expedition ; secondly, of men who died while building the railway which proved the key to Lord Kitchener's success ; thirdly, of soldiers who perished in the war of 1898 ; lastly, of civil servants who have died while administering the country since its reconquest.

Staveacre and I touched a much earlier phase of history when we discovered and bought derelict French helmets and cuirasses of 1798 that must once have been the booty of some Mameluke. Who would wish for more romantic trophies ?

The Turkish war added gravity to the Battalion's responsibilities in the Sudan. The idea at the time was to treat it passively, so long as the Turks did not molest British Moslems on pilgrimage to Mecca. The Arabs were known to have little sympathy with the Ottoman Turk and his pretensions to religious authority ; so Jiddah was not to be starved by non-intercourse. The Turks themselves made such a policy impossible by their raid against the Suez Canal in February, 1915, and the inception of the Dardanelles Expedition marked the final victory of the school of thought which put its faith in an Eastern offensive. Some sort of offensive, whether against Gallipoli or Alexandretta or Haifa, had become perhaps a moral necessity.

We learnt in the Sudan how Turco-German machinations were necessitating a more active policy towards the Porte. I acted as prosecutor at the public trial of a Sudanese by general court martial in the court-house of Port Sudan in the second week of December, 1914. He had risen from sergeant's rank in a Sudanese regiment to be Captain of the Egyptian Coastguard in 1907. Cashiered in 1912, he served Enver Pasha in Tripoli, became an officer of Abdul Hamid's bodyguard, and afterwards a Major of the Baghdad Gendarmerie. Long before November, 1914, he had busily plotted for a rising in Egypt and the diffusion of German propaganda all over the Sudan. Under Enver Pasha's personal direction he disguised himself in a pilgrim's robe, styled himself Suleiman Effendi, and crossed the Red Sea from Jiddah with six pilgrims. One of these was an Howrowri Arab from Kordofan. The rest were Falatas or Takruri—*i.e.* pilgrims from British West Africa to Mecca—a class whose whole existence is spent on pilgrimage, brightened by spells

THE SUDAN

of residence and family life at centres like Omdurman, and this man planned to pass as a pilgrim among pilgrims. The party was asked by the sheikh of the Takurna village, near Port Sudan, where they came from. They replied: "Omdurman." On the 16th November he, in beggar's clothes, sought an interview with a Bimbashi of the Egyptian Army, at Port Sudan. He told him and his adjutant that he had come on a secret mission from Enver to rouse the Sudan against the British and to ascertain native feeling at Port Sudan, Khartum, Sinja, Wad Medani, Kordofan and El Obeid.

"The Porte," he said, "knows that the English treat you badly and intends to drive them out of Egypt." The officers whom he tempted were, however, staunchly loyal. They handed him over to Colonel Wilson, Governor of the Red Sea Province. His red and blue uniform, sword and papers were discovered, but he defended himself stoutly against the charges of spying and war treason, and his interests were carefully watched by Judge Davidson, who acted as Judge Advocate. One Arabic letter found among his papers was addressed to the Ministry of War at Constantinople, and appears to have been a copy of a report sent off by him just before his arrest. It is worth quoting as a footnote to history:

"I arrived at Mecca, where I met the Valy and Commandant, Wahib Bey, and gave him my information. He left Mecca for Jiddah at once for his usual work, and provided me with a boat and six civilians, who accompanied me from Jiddah to Suakin and Port Sudan on a secret mission to induce the natives to favour the presence of the Turkish government, to rise against the existing European government, and to take necessary precautions for upholding the honour of the Turkish government without anyone's knowledge. . . . I hope when I reach Khartum, in a secret way to encourage a rising against the British troops, if possible. As for my expenses, I took from the Valy Commandant sixteen Turkish pounds and three pounds sterling for the necessary expenses of the journey by steamer and land. I have every wish for the prosperity of the Religion and for the Sultan's victory over the unbelievers."

This man in his defence denied that any Sudanese like himself would dream of plotting against the British, who had purified government, employed Sudanese in administration, and given their children schools. He was convicted and sentenced to death, but that penalty was commuted by the Sirdar, in consideration of a tardy confession.

One of the Falatas turned King's evidence against his other companions on the charge of war treason. Squatting on the floor of the courthouse, their rosaries interlaced with their handcuffs, they assumed the air of innocence, but were convicted and condemned to terms of imprisonment. Two were called Isa (Jesus) and one was

THE SUDAN

Adam. Arab life has more than a touch of the Bible.

The whole episode brought into relief the wide ramifications of Turco-German intrigue.

Another singular case of German subtlety was that of an alleged Swiss explorer, who arrived on the 10th November at Khartum on his way from Abyssinia to undergo the Pasteur treatment at Cairo. He claimed to have had his leg bitten by a dog, and was in hot haste to reach Egypt. He satisfied our doctors as to the genuineness of his injuries and anxiety, wept when Captain Morley, most expert of surgeons, told him of the surrender of Antwerp, and was given help and hospitality. He went through the Pasteur treatment and disappeared from our ken. A few weeks later an Italian newspaper applauded the patriotism of a German reserve officer, whose zeal to serve his country had nerved him to brave the vigilance of Khartum and the too devoted attentions of the hydrophobia experts at Cairo.

At a date when all Britons of military age worth their salt were training for war, the actual work of the Manchesters in the Sudan hardly calls for description. In the personal supervision of the Sirdar they enjoyed a special advantage not shared by the Territorial units left in Egypt. What is of more lasting moment is the share they took in furthering the cause of peace, order and good government in the Sudan by their steady conduct and happy relations with the inhabitants. Our officers interchanged visits with the officers of an Egyptian regiment quartered at Khartum, enjoying tea, music and speeches. With an Egyptian regiment at El Obeid we had a pleasant and symbolic exchange of colours. In the ceremonial occasioned by the Sultan's accession, a guard of honour under Major J. H. Staveacre represented the British Army in the Palace garden, and acclaimed: "Ya-aish Hussein Pasha, Sultan Masr" (Long live Hussein Pasha, Sultan of Egypt). The men were scrupulously careful of native sensibilities. At Port Sudan, Private J. P. Lyons, our champion boxer, who was killed on Gallipoli, was publicly thanked by the Governor, Colonel Wilson, for having saved a black policeman from some drunken sailors. The Battalion hoped it had really earned the honour paid it when the Sirdar accepted its honorary colonelcy.

The knowledge gained during the months in the Sudan will be an asset to such Manchester Territorials as survive, and may even exercise an influence upon local public opinion. To many, the Sudan seemed entitled to rank among the best administered countries in the world. Its civil service governs vast areas and vast numbers practically without military aid. Its selection from University graduates who best combine brains with physique is in the spirit of Cecil Rhodes. Government of blacks by whites is a commonplace; of blacks by blues, a stroke of genius.

Looking back after years of soldiering and

disillusion, the first months of the War no doubt seem brighter than they really were. It is easy to forget the illnesses that sent the writer as an invalid to Luxor and Cairo, and finally to England ; to ignore the heat and dust and isolation, the long glare of the African day. We think more readily of Gordon's rose-tree blooming in the Palace garden ; of the long camel treks across the desert ; of the wail of the yellow-ribboned Sudanese bagpipes ; of our visit with Colonel Smyth, V.C., to the stony, sun-baked battle-field of Omdurman ; of the lusty strains of *Tipperary* in the cool barrack rooms. It is right that this should be so. The men to whom these memories would appeal were men who enjoyed life to the full. They played the first lacrosse ever seen in the Sudan, engaged in keen boxing competitions, rallied to football on the roughest of barrack squares, listened cheerfully to weekly concerts and the first of our long series of history and military lectures. They hunted for curios in the dusty alleys of Omdurman, enjoyed recreation in the library and billiard-room, and ran with great spirit the early numbers of the *Manchester Sentry*, first published of all active service periodicals. To this paper the Sirdar and Lady Wingate contributed welcome and inspiring letters, and the Battalion owed its motto : " We never sleep."

In April, 1915, the Battalion left the Sudan for Cairo, where it again came in contact with the other units of the East Lancashire Territorial Division, thenceforward called the 42nd Division

On the 3rd May it embarked in company with another battalion of the Manchesters on the *Ionian*, and at seven in the evening, on the 7th May, it landed at "V" Beach, Cape Helles.

CHAPTER III

GALLIPOLI

THE 42nd Division was soon in the midst of hard fighting, stormy weather and much privation. Casualties began early, though the first Battalion exploit under fire was happily bloodless. On the 9th May, 80 men were told off to fill water-bottles and carry them under fire over half-a-mile of broken ground to an Australian unit. They tracked cleverly across the moor, and were met by an eager Australian with the question: "Have you brought the water, cobbers?" On the 11th, the Battalion had a long, weary march to the front line. The trenches were full of water, and the gullies became almost impassable. On the 28th, Lockwood, our musketry expert, was severely wounded in the chest.

On the same day Lieutenant-Colonel Gresham was forced by ill-health to leave us. He was invalided to Malta, and thence to England. A year later he relinquished his command, without having been able to rejoin. He had served with the Battalion ever since 1890. He was known to suffer from chronic illness, but he let nothing interfere with the call of duty, and his hard work overseas set a fine example to all ranks. It is, indeed, still, in 1917, difficult to think of the Battalion with any other Commanding Officer. His departure was widely regretted, and the later achievements of his men in the War are the best tribute to the many years of labour he had given to their training and organisation.

His immediate successor in command was Major Staveacre. On the night of the 28th May the Battalion advanced, and B and D Companies dug themselves in under a full moon and in the face of the enemy, a platoon of C Company finishing the work on the following evening. In these operations fell Captains T. W. Savatard and R. V. Rylands, men of sterling character and capacity, and Lieut. T. F. Brown, a gallant boy, who, in the happier days of the threatened war in Ulster, had served in the West Belfast Loyalist Volunteers.

The advance of the 28th May was preliminary to the historic attack of the whole allied line from sea to sea, which had been timed for midday on the 4th June 1915. In this attack the Battalion advanced as the extreme right unit of our Infantry Brigade. On the left of the Manchesters was the 29th Division; on our right was the Royal Naval Division, and on their right were the French.

During the previous night the Turks, writes an eyewitness in the *Sentry*, gave us " our first taste of bombing. They crawled down a small gully and threw eight or nine bombs on to our gun emplacement, hurting no one, but putting the gun

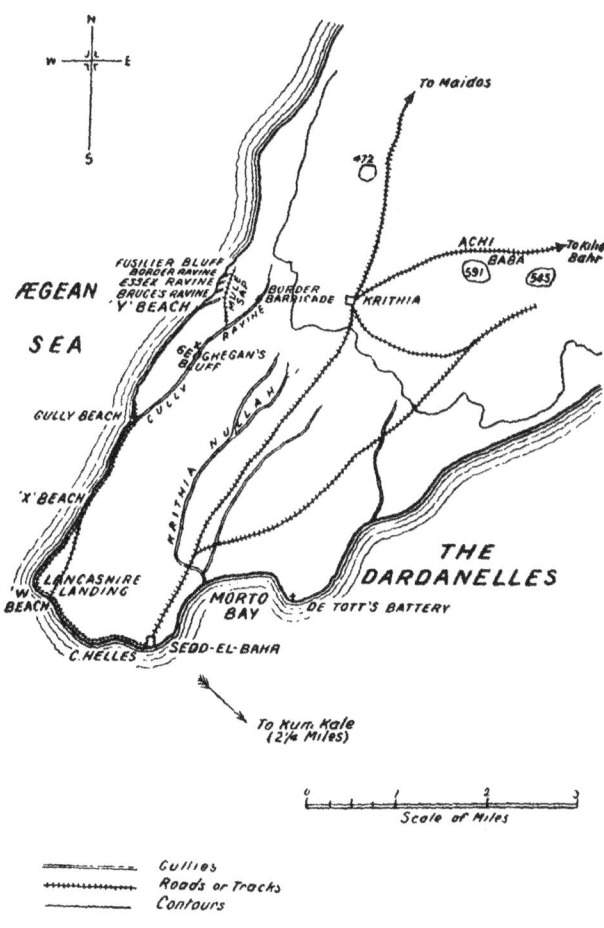

GALLIPOLI.

GALLIPOLI

out for twenty minutes." Meanwhile they fired the gorse in front of the 29th Division.

At eight in the morning the British guns opened the bombardment. "At eleven-twenty our whole line from the sea to the Straits got up and waved their bayonets, pretending the attack was to start." At twelve, "with wild cheers" the assault was launched. A and C Companies rushed the first Turkish trench, and captured the surviving occupants, while along a front that stretched far away to the left, similar success was won by the whole British line. While A and C Companies consolidated the trench they had won, B and D Companies passed over it, in order to take the next Turkish line. Captain (afterwards Major) C. E. Higham, always resourceful and imperturbable, was shot in the foot while crossing the trench, but Captain (afterwards Lieutenant-Colonel) Fawcus led the attack a long way forward, and held a dummy trench in the heart of the Turkish position for many hours.

Subsequently the right flank of the Battalion was not only enfiladed but exposed to fire from their rear. The officers at this deadly point were Lieutenants H. D. Thewlis, W. G. Freemantle and F. C. Palmer. Palmer was badly wounded. Thewlis, a keen subaltern and expert in scientific agriculture, refused to retire, and was killed. Freemantle was of Quaker stock and, like Thewlis, a graduate of Manchester University. He was first shot through the right arm, and then through the left. He insisted on remaining with his men, though the pain was so intense that he broke his teeth while clenching them. He was then shot through the body, and died.

C Company on this right flank was in danger. Lieutenant G. C. Hans Hamilton, a prince of fighters, had organised a bombing party with Corporal Cherry, and did great work, but was now severely wounded. Leonard Dudley, an adventurous soul who had fought under Staveacre with the Cheshire Yeomanry in South Africa, was killed. Captain Cyril Norbury, who commanded the Company, had written to Major Staveacre for information, and he received this answer from Captain Creagh : " Regret to say Major Staveacre dead ; also Thewlis and Freemantle. Do not know whereabouts of missing platoons. Fear most lost."

Staveacre had been shot through the back while passing ammunition to the firing line. He said to Regimental Sergeant-Major H. C. Franklin (the Acting Adjutant of our later days on Gallipoli): " Never mind me. Carry on, Sergeant-Major," and died at once.

All day long the Turks counter-attacked the Manchesters without success. Private Richardson won the D.C.M. by bombing feats, but the supply of bombs ran out early. Their use was in its infancy, and their character was primitive. C Company, among whom Sergeant M'Hugh, Corporal Basnett and Private (afterwards Lieutenant) J. W. Sutherland were conspicuous, was reinforced by some gallant bombers from another battalion of the Manchesters under

GALLIPOLI

Captain James, who was killed after driving the Turks from a trench, and later by some of the Lancashire Fusiliers. They held their own, and a last Turkish counter-attack, on the morning of the 5th June, was scattered by our machine guns and those of the Lancashire Fusiliers, well handled by Captains Hayes and Bedson.

Fawcus brought back about nine survivors from his advanced position after great feats of endurance, in which the Manchester units on our left had fully shared. Lieutenant T. E. Granger, who had been left behind dangerously wounded, was taken prisoner. Lieutenant Ward was killed. Lieutenant Bateman was shot through the lungs; Lieutenant G. Norbury on the scalp.

On the 4th June the Brigadier, General Noel Lee, was mortally wounded, to the intense and universal sorrow of the whole Division. He died in Malta. Lieutenant-Colonel Heys, on taking his place, was immediately killed. The retreat from the more advanced trenches to the original Turkish firing line, necessitated by enfilade fire and by the absence of reinforcements, proved far deadlier than the advance. The battle, with its preliminary operations, cost us some of our bravest sergeant-majors and sergeants—Cookson, Arnott, Marvin, Mundy, Balfe, Webster. Sergeant Lindsay lost his leg. Of them and of all the men of the 42nd Division, who gave their lives in this action, any praise is superfluous.

A broad strip of land gained securely on a wide frontage, an immense number of Turkish dead and prisoners, and a sense of great personal ascendancy, were the measure of their success, and General Sir Ian Hamilton's dispatch truly estimates its quality.

The survivors of the Battalion rested for a few days on Imbros after the battle, and then returned to the Peninsula under the command of Captain P. H. Creagh. On the 16th July the command was passed to Lieutenant-Colonel A. Canning, a veteran of the Egyptian War of 1882, who had previously commanded the Leinster Regiment at Cork. We could have had no greater confidence in any possible Commanding Officer, and while he acted as Brigadier of the Manchester Territorials his influence was no less inspiring. The record of our later campaign on Gallipoli is closely associated with his name and work.

All these early scenes of the expedition to the Dardanelles I had missed. On the 17th March I had been invalided home on the Indian hospital ship, *Glenart Castle*, Alexandria to Southampton, and the only public meeting I witnessed during three years of warfare—a recruiting rally in the Manchester Hippodrome—was a poor outlet for one's activity. An offer of the command of the new 3rd line reserve unit at Southport naturally failed to quench my keenness to rejoin the Battalion, and after vexatious delays I at last sailed from Devonport for the East, on the *Simla*, on the 13th July 1915.

We reached Alexandria on the 25th, and the crowded harbour of Mudros early on the 29th.

The boat was full of drafts for the 29th Division—
Essex and Hampshire men, Inniskillings, Munsters,
Royal and Lancashire Fusiliers, Worcesters—and
rumours of the intended Suvla expedition were in
the air. Our optimism was, however, chastened
by the opinions of one experienced soldier on
board, who insisted that we ought never to have
landed at Cape Helles, but on the Gulf of Saros
behind the lines of Bulair, and made straight for
Constantinople with a large army, without trying
to force the Dardanelles. He believed that the
Germans would still take Warsaw, and thought
Holland's co-operation essential to any plan of
early success. The War was still at a stage when
men did not mind talking about it, and the general
assumption was that it could not last long. One
sailor told me a story typical of the German's
ignorance of sportsmanship. A captured naval
officer was courteously allowed the use of the
British captain's cabin. A few moments later
a crash announced that he had requited chivalry
by breaking everything he could lay his hands on.
Other passengers on the *Simla* were nursing sisters
in dainty scarlet and grey, naval airmen who
disembarked at Valetta, and the whole staff of
an Australian General Hospital bound for Mudros
—expert specialist officers and splendid men,
with songs cheery and robust :

"When the beer's on the table, we'll be there."

Perhaps my most vivid memories, however, are
of the keen young officers conducting drafts, who

were so soon to fall in the great attempt at Suvla.

The fate of one of these, J. R. Lingard, then in charge of some Lancashire Fusiliers, was one of the unsolved mysteries of the Dardanelles campaign. A brave and popular officer, he was severely wounded on the 21st August. He was carried out of action and placed on a stretcher for conveyance across Suvla Beach to a hospital ship. At this point all trace of him disappeared. His fate is unknown.

In the late afternoon of the 30th July 1915 we neared Cape Helles and heard the thunder of the guns. We landed laboriously about midnight, and were led by guides to a rendezvous of the 29th Division at a point some three miles along the coast on the northern side of the Peninsula. Brilliant moonlight shone upon a sleeping French force close to the landing-place on "V" Beach. The country looked unspeakably dry and bare.

At six o'clock the following morning we were divided into details for our various units, and sleepless, unshaven and hungry, I was again guided to where the 42nd Division had its headquarters—a spot to the south of the 29th, and, roughly, in the left centre of the short line of the Allies. The narrowness and shallowness of the area of our occupation struck all observers at once. The great ridge of Achi Baba, some six hundred feet above sea-level, barring our advance upon Turkey, confronted us the very moment that we climbed to the top of the cliffs that enclosed every landing-place. We were shelled as we struck across the moorland, and then I found myself once more in East Lancashire.

A long wait at Divisional Headquarters was followed by a delightful welcome at the Quartermaster's dump of the Battalion, where, in blazing sunshine, I enjoyed my first food and shave on enemy soil, and abundant news of the unit. A friendly sergeant then led me up to the fire trenches some two miles forward, where the Manchesters held both sides of Krithia nullah, a ravine running up into a sloping heath, where the Turks had lain dug in for the last two months. Our way, after passing "Clapham Junction," was fringed with the graves of the fallen. I noticed Staveacre's.

It was pleasant to reach the cool burrow, which served as our Battalion Headquarters. Here I found Colonel Canning, P. H. Creagh and Fawcus sitting on the yellow, dusty ground beneath a tarpaulin. It was thrilling once again to walk among our Manchester men, now very thin and sunburnt, in shirt-sleeves and shorts, making the best of life in narrow trenches, and watching day after day the serried Turkish lines and broad, brown mass of Achi Baba. Next day (1st August), in mid-afternoon, we moved into the most advanced fire trenches, and I became O.C. of our Battalion's firing line, with a small dug-out of my own in the centre of our sector. This sector was within forty or fifty yards of the Turkish position, and in the early morning, as the sun rose over Asia, we heard the *muezzin* calling the faithful to prayer. There was a lull at this time in warfare. Casualties were few, and the periscope disclosed little beyond the vista (soon too familiar) of arid heath, broken only by patches of wild thyme, and of the intricate lacework of sandbagged trenches stretching from the tip of Cape Helles behind us to the top of Achi Baba. But for the constant booming of the guns and the plague of flies, these first days on Gallipoli were days of peace and happiness under a quiet, blue sky. Our men were hopeful, and a stray memorandum of mine of the 3rd August records that " P. H. Creagh bets Fawcus £1 that the Turks will be driven out of the Peninsula within a month." Our faith was great in those days.

CHAPTER IV

THE AUGUST BATTLES AT CAPE HELLES

IN the history of the expedition to the Dardanelles, the August battles in the area of Cape Helles figure as a pinning or holding attack by the British Army, designed to occupy the enemy while the Suvla Bay landing was effected. The line of communications that linked the Achi Baba position with Maidos and Gallipoli was to be cut by our forces operating from Suvla and Anzac, and the Narrows were to be opened to our fleet by the capture of Sari-Bair. The epic of the actual Suvla effort has been nobly told in both Sir Ian Hamilton's dispatches and Mr Masefield's *Gallipoli*.

The Regimental officer at Cape Helles naturally knew very little of the strategy underlying these operations, and nothing of events at Suvla or Anzac, though Suvla was but thirteen miles and Anzac but five from Fusilier Bluff. His could only be the impressions of an eyewitness in an orbit limited to his Brigade. During the whole of our Gallipoli experiences, we were only conscious of Divisional organisation and personnel through the literature and correspondence of the orderly-room, or from mere glimpses on the occasion of our rare visits to the base on Gully Beach. I am glad to have once seen the Commander-in-Chief, Sir Ian Hamilton. He passed our Headquarters on the Western Mule Sap, walking briskly towards the trenches. The fine appreciation of the Manchester Territorial Brigade's work on the 4th June, which he wrote in his dispatches, made his name a name always to conjure with, but to the man in the trenches, an Army Commander can at most be but a shining name. Consequently, the story of the fighting in August, as we saw it, must needs be silent on all vexed questions of high policy, and also on the more famous struggle to the north of Achi Baba. Its limitations are true to life.

On the 5th August we learnt that our Army was to assault the enemy's position simultaneously with the enterprise at Suvla.

Three points were emphasised in our instructions. First, the frontage and depth of the sector to be carried by each unit was carefully and personally explained to us by General the Hon. H. A. Lawrence, who was at that time our Brigadier. Secondly, we had to tell our men that the Turkish lines would have been rendered almost untenable before their advance, in consequence of the heavy bombardment, which was to precede the attack. Thirdly, we were to emphasise to the men that Turkish morale was on the wane. Prisoners, whose only words were " English good ; Turkey finish," were, I fancy, responsible for this last venture in optimism.

We had every reason to anticipate that the attempt was to be a thorough onslaught, not a mere demonstration, and would probably lead to success. The discovery that the Turks had in reality been massing for an attack on our lines within a few hours of our own assault was only made afterwards.

At 2.20 P.M. on the 6th August, the British guns opened on the Turkish positions in front of the 29th Division, and at 3.50 P.M. we could see our infantry advance under a hail of musketry and machine-gun fire. Our guns lengthened range, and we saw shells fired by our warships in the Gulf of Saros bursting along the crest of Achi Baba. Through the periscope we watched the tin back-plates, worn by our men for the enlightenment of artillery observers, twinkling under the dust and smoke. Some other Manchesters were lending a hand in the battle already, and were struggling under heavy shrapnel fire to gain a footing in the trenches immediately to the north of the sector to be assaulted by the Brigade on the morrow. Then gradually the firing sank. By 4.45 P.M. there was a distinct lull. One of our Companies (C Company) under Captain G. Chadwick, was sent as reinforcements. A stream of wounded (Manchesters, Worcesters, Munsters) began to file past our lines into the winding nullah. We knew little as to what had happened. The sky above the shell-riddled ridge of Achi Baba was serene and purple in the glow of evening, but the fog of war was upon us.

Suddenly, at 6.40 P.M., a message came that two of our Companies were required at once to help the Worcester Regiment, who had taken part in the assault about a mile to the north of where we were. A Company (Captain A. E. F. Fawcus) and D Company (Captain H. Smedley) were ordered to comply. The men were resting for the work planned for the next day. They got ready hurriedly, and moved in fast-gathering darkness along a labyrinth of unfamiliar trenches to a position from which the Worcesters had advanced in the afternoon.

Our information was most vague. The Worcesters had gone " over the top " many hours earlier and had disappeared. They were believed to be holding trenches somewhere beyond, but they were out of touch with our line, and it was intended to reinforce them. The night was dark, and the direction to be taken after leaving our trenches could only be roughly indicated. A Company lined up first, and went over the top like one man. D Company, which was to move to the right of A, then lined up along the fire step and followed.

Our men passed into a tornado of fire, and drifted forward on a broken moor, already littered with dead and wounded. Both Companies eventually lined up in shallow depressions of ground, but there was no trench to receive them.

Meanwhile, many of our wounded had straggled back to the trench from which they started, and numbers of wounded Regulars of the 29th Division who had lain out for many hours were brought in by our men during the long night. This was the one bright touch in its story. We laid down these brave men on the narrow fire-step, and our stretcher-bearers worked nobly. Several men went out with stretchers under heavy fire, and fetched in as many survivors as they could find. One, I remember, was called Corris. At midnight the Colonel and Captain P. H. Creagh, our Adjutant, left for Headquarters, where the morrow's plan of operations was being partially recast. The hours passed. At last two messengers clambered back with reports from Fawcus and Smedley. Lance-Corporal H. L. MacCartney brought the former's.

The only sensible course was for our parties to come in. I noticed that MacCartney's hand was broken and bleeding, and suggested to him that someone else should go back with my message of recall. He insisted on his ability to go, and with a companion he climbed over the parapet. A few moments later he was shot through the heart. Smedley's messenger was Lance-Corporal G. W. F. Franklin, whose services on the field won him a commission, and who played a splendid part in the subsequent annals of the Battalion. He was given a like message of recall for Captain Smedley, and with it he too clambered back over the parapet and passed out into the night.

At 3.30 A.M. on the 7th August the two Companies toiled homewards, having lost heavily.

Davidson, a plucky Australian officer attached to us, was among the killed. He had been in charge of a working party which wandered in the darkness into the Turkish lines, and was there destroyed.

After a couple of hours' sleep, we rose to take our part in the renewed offensive. A heavy bombardment was to precede a general advance. As the front-line trenches lay within a few yards of the Turks, they were now practically cleared of men in order to avoid casualties from our own gun-fire. The scheme laid down for our Battalion required a north-east advance by C and B Companies out of the narrow defile known as Krithia nullah. A gap was therefore made overnight in the barrier that had hitherto crossed the mouth of the defile and linked our fire trenches with those neighbouring. A machine gun was placed at the north-west corner of this gap under cover of the end of our fire trench. On the south-east side of the gap, a barricade ran up a steep slope to the trenches of other Manchesters, whose assault was to be simultaneous with ours. Owing to the clearance of the fire trenches, the assaulting parties had, unfortunately, to move across the open. The nullah was twisted and partly covered by curving banks on either flank; so that it was hoped that our men might nevertheless avoid complete exposure. The great hope, however, was that the British guns would succeed in wrecking the redoubt that commanded the outlet of the nullah before the infantry moved.

We waited at the spot where the support line ran down to the nullah and from which C Company was to emerge, while our artillery thundered against the enemy's position. Then the hour came, and C Company, under Chadwick (bravest of the brave), moved in single file into the nullah and onward towards the gap in the front-line barricade and the Turkish redoubt beyond.

B Company, under Captain J. R. Creagh, followed in their wake.

At the same time a battalion of the Manchesters, commanded by Lieut.-Col. Darlington, was launched against the Turkish line on the left of the redoubt, and another, under Lieut.-Col. Pilkington, against the line on its right. The redoubt itself was at the apex of a broad angle of trenches.

It was at once obvious that our guns had been unable to affect the strength and resisting power of the enemy's front line. Each advancing wave of the Manchesters was swept away by machine-gun fire. A few of them gallantly reached the Turkish trenches and fell there. Long afterwards, during the last flicker of a British offensive in December, some Lowland Scots soldiers of the 52nd Division found in trenches on the west of the nullah the bodies of some of the Manchester men, who had also this day fought a way to their objective and perished.

We saw shrapnel bursting along the nullah, through which C Company was passing, and progress seemed stopped. I ran along the deserted saps that connected our support line with the front firing trench, and came to the gap. Some twenty yards ahead, a group of about thirty men were lying together in the shallow water-course, mostly dead. Another group was gathered under cover by the gap. The rest of C and B Companies were still running up to the gap from the support line through the long grass of the nullah, and dropping in their tracks under the constant fire of the redoubt. Chadwick and J. R. Creagh were both in the forefront of the advance, and Chadwick signalled back its hopelessness. His subaltern, Bacon, had been the first to pass the gap, and had been killed on emerging. The whole battle in this sector was really over, and I stopped the men under cover from moving out into the open. In the late afternoon the survivors of the little group in front crawled back to safety. The dead were gathered in by the devoted stretcher-bearers under Sergeant Mort, during the evening. One party, under Corporal F. White, had alone penetrated to within a few yards of the redoubt. He held his men together through the afternoon and brought them in under cover of darkness, for which the D.C.M. was his reward. Mort had won the D.C.M. earlier in the campaign.

All through that hot afternoon the wounded Manchesters trailed back to the busy dressing-stations, pictures of suffering and patience. The attack still further reduced the numbers of the original Territorial units, already greatly diminished by casualties.

In Khartum Station.
Col. Gresham.   General Wingate.

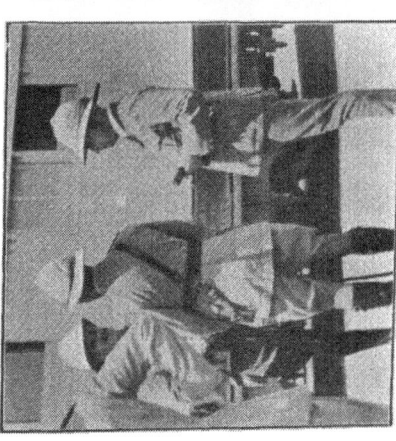

In the Turkish trench captured on 4th June.

We wondered to what extent the effort at Cape Helles had eased the great task of the armies operating from Anzac and Suvla Bay. The guns used to boom all day long from the hidden north until the 22nd August, when the attempt was given up. Several weeks passed before we realised that the valiant armies there had laboured in vain, and that Sari-Bair had remained unconquered.

We were far more conscious of the limited results of the battle on the Cape Helles side of Achi Baba.

To the right of the line attacked by the Manchester Brigade and some 200 yards east of Krithia nullah, the Lancashire Fusiliers succeeded, with great gallantry, in capturing a small plot known as the Vineyard, which the Turks in six days' hard fighting were unable to regain.

Regarded purely as a holding attack during the main enterprise from Suvla, the offensive fully achieved its purpose. It was, however, difficult to look upon it in this somewhat narrow light from the point of view of a Regiment which took part in the actual adventure.

Of the many personalities that struck one's imagination during this August battle, the majority were simply of the rank and file, whose pluck and unselfishness were incomparable. Of most I have forgotten the very names. There was a postman from Bradford, who was forty-seven years old and had thirteen children. I remember his telling me of South African experiences. He fell. Most of our men were far younger. Many were mere boys, whose days in the Camel Corps at Khartum had been their first taste of manhood. Their Company Sergeant-Major, Leigh, was mortally wounded by shrapnel while running up the nullah.

Of our officers, Captains Smedley and Chadwick survived to be pillars of strength during the whole campaign. About the time when I finally left the unit Captain Smedley joined the Egyptian Army as a Bimbashi, and Chadwick the Royal Flying Corps. Chadwick received a Serbian decoration.

Fawcus, who distinguished himself by his cool leadership on the night of the 6th August, left the Battalion very soon afterwards to conduct a newly formed Bombing School on the Peninsula. He was the recipient of many well-earned honours, and ultimately, as a battalion commander, won wider fame in another theatre of war.

A number of the men received cards from Divisional Headquarters, expressing appreciation of their gallantry: Sergeants W. Harrison and M'Hugh; Corporal (afterwards Company Sergeant-Major) J. Joyce; Lance-Corporal (afterwards Lieutenant) G. W. F. Franklin; Lance-Corporal (afterwards Lieutenant) W. T. Thorp; Corporals Hulme and Cherry; Privates Anderson, Beckett, Bradbury, Fletcher, Hayes, Hamilton, Maher, Murphy and Walsh. Joyce was afterwards awarded the Russian Order of St George.

On the 15th August 1915 we were relieved by a Lowland Scots Brigade of the 52nd Division, and moved to what were then called the Scotch dug-outs, a bivouac about two and a half miles behind the fire trenches upon the central plateau of the Peninsula. It was hot and dusty, but five minutes' walk led the weary to the cliff. We used to go down its steep side on to the coast road, full of soldiers of the Allied Armies, of carts and mules with long tassel fly protectors, and of Indian or Zionist muleteers. Across the road a lighter was moored, from which we bathed happily in a peaceful sea, with the pale blue contours of Imbros and Samothrace cut clearly against the sky, and our trawlers and cruisers moving up and down on their ceaseless watch between Cape Helles and Anzac. Here and here alone was it possible to forget the brown wilderness above the cliff, and all the toil and bloodshed between ourselves and the summit of Achi Baba.

Casualties are soon forgotten in war. In the dusty and exposed dug-outs, which were now our refuge, men revived. After the recent losses, it was good to see our clever Territorials transforming what looked like dog biscuits into a palatable porridge, cooking rice and raisins, picking lice from their grey woollen shirts, reading papers (all very light and very old), grumbling, but ever cheerful. It was in the Scotch dug-outs that we heard of the loss of the *Royal Edward* and of the German entry into Warsaw; but already mails and food held the first place in our minds. Man readjusts his sense of proportion as he enters a theatre of war.

On the 19th August, Colonel Canning became

temporary Brigadier. I thus became Commanding Officer in his absence. The same day we left our bivouac, and after a long, hot, march, through the dusty gorge called Gully Ravine, we relieved another unit in the firing line on the northerly side of that great artery of British life and traffic.

CHAPTER V

TRENCH WARFARE ON GALLIPOLI

THE routine upon which the Battalion entered at this stage remained almost unchanged until the evacuation. Our Headquarters, where I slept when in command of the Battalion during Colonel Canning's various short spells as acting Brigadier, were usually in some heather-covered gorge, opening upon a deep blue sea. Essex Ravine was a frequent site. The side of this ravine which faced the north-east protruded beyond the side sheltered from the Turkish fire, and was thus forbidden ground. All down the slope were spread the dismembered remains of hundreds of Turks, who must have been slaughtered in retreat by guns from our warships in the Ægean Sea. It was impossible to bury them, owing to the enemy's fire. The other side, where we slept on a rocky ledge high above the sea, was still a beautiful glen.

An hour before dawn we went round the lines, while the men " stood to." We returned for a bathe and breakfast in the open, while the destroyers used to pass to and fro between Cape Helles and the Gulf of Saros, and a pearly haze brooded over Imbros. Then back to the trenches, which were always dusty and fly-pestered, to visit men always under fire, but full of bravery and patience. Diarrhœa and dysentery were already sending many of them from the Peninsula. The trenches were often noisome. Only in the evening, with Imbros growing fainter in the fading day and Samothrace rising huge and cloudy behind, while the red and green lights of the hospital ships off Helles shone brightly across the water, was physical vigour possible. When I acted as Second in Command, as was more usual, my nights were spent in the centre of the firing line, with excellent telephonists like Hoyle or Clavering close to me, but the nights were usually quiet, and indeed it was not until the middle of September that the Turks showed any symptoms of the offensive spirit. Our casualties were mainly caused by random shots at night, which chanced to hit our sentries as they peered into the gloom over the parapet.

After a fortnight's spell in the trenches, rest bivouacs were welcome as a change, though the name was a mere mockery. Mining and loading fatigues were incessant. I admired the humour of a Wigan sergeant, whom I heard encouraging a gang of perspiring soldiers, while carrying heavy ammunition boxes up a hill-side one sweltering afternoon, with the incitement that they must " Remember Belgium."

For a Field Officer one of the most trying experiences of such breaks in the common routine was the task of presiding over field general courts-martial. Courts-martial under peace con-

TRENCH WARFARE ON GALLIPOLI 47

ditions are not without interest to a lawyer, but these in the field dealt wholly with grave charges, such as falling asleep while on sentry duty and other offences almost as dangerous and considerably more heinous morally. It was hard in many cases to reconcile the exigencies of war with the call of humanity, and the sense of responsibility was only partially relieved by the knowledge that a higher authority would give due weight to the extenuating circumstances that appealed so often to one's compassion. The introduction of "suspended sentences" by the Army (Suspension of Sentences) Act 1915, with a view to keep a man's rifle in the firing line, and to give an offender the chance of retrieving his liberty by subsequent devotion to duty, was probably the War's best addition to British Military Law. Nevertheless, the duty of acting as President on these occasions is found universally distasteful.

There were, however, two great charms in these short intervals in trench warfare. First, it was delightful to escape to places where you could move erect and see something besides the brown wilderness of saps and cuts. A walk to Lancashire Landing along the coast road, between great rugged cliffs on one side and the rippling sea on the other, took us past the little colony of the Greek Labour Corps, and past terraces of new stone huts and sandbag dug-outs, which indicated the presence of Staff Officers. Looking seaward, we saw the hull of the sunken *Majestic*, a perpetual sign of the limitations of "sea power." We could then strike up from the beach and see the A.S.C. stores, admirably managed by Major (afterwards Lieutenant-Colonel) A. England, and pushing on to the top of the plateau, the whole area of warfare between Lancashire Landing and Achi Baba was at our feet.

Even more delightful was the long series of entertainments which we organised in the Battalion, and which eventually drew large numbers from the rest of the 42nd Division. These entertainments were opened by lectures on history. Our men became familiar with the history and conditions of all the belligerent Powers, and were kept well acquainted with the developments of the actual military situation in Europe. They enjoyed these lectures. Education has its uses, after all. Then followed concerts, which were splendidly arranged by Regimental Sergeant-Major M. Hartnett, a veteran of Ladysmith and East Africa and a pillar of the Battalion, now, alas, dead, and by Quartermaster-Sergeant Mort, himself an adept as an entertainer. These "shows" used to start about 6.45 in the evening, and the vision of our tired boys scattered in the fast fading twilight on the slope of some narrow ravine beneath the serene, starry sky of Turkey will be among our most lasting memories of Gallipoli. The sentimental song was typical of the Territorial's taste. Even now I can hear the refrain sung by Company Sergeant-Major J. W. Woods:

> "My heart's far away with the Colleen I adore;
> Eileen alannah; Angus asthor."

TRENCH WARFARE ON GALLIPOLI 49

At the finish, before singing the National Anthem and the no less popular anthem of the Machine Gun Section, our men always sang : *Keep the Home Fires Burning.* The soldiers could have no better vesper hymn.

On the 8th September 1915 we went into a new sector of trenches on either side of what was called Border Barricade. The name was, like Border Ravine, a relic of the Border Regiment, just as Skinner's Lane, Watling Street, Essex Ravine and Inniskilling Inch recalled the activities of other units.

I can claim personal responsibility for placing Burlington Street and Greenheys Lane upon the map of Gallipoli. They are reminders of our Headquarters in Manchester.

Border Barricade barred a moorland track which led upwards to higher ground where the Turks were strongly entrenched. Below it were little graveyards of Turkish and British dead, and below them the moors contracted into the narrow defile of Gully Ravine. Here on the 15th September we lost some casualties in a mine explosion, which the Turks had carefully timed for our evening's "Stand to." Dense columns of smoke and earth shot up high into the air, and the rapidly increasing darkness of the evening added greatly to our difficulties. Most gallant work was done in digging out buried men, a task of great danger, as the front trench was completely destroyed, and the Turks, whose trenches at this point were within ten yards of ours, were bombing heavily. Thirteen men lost their lives through the explosion. For some days afterwards this spot and an open space behind it were constantly sniped, and, as an addition to our troubles, one of our own trench mortars, fired by a neighbouring unit, landed in error in our lines, killing 3 men and wounding 4, including Captain Smedley. Later the Turks exploded further mines in the same area when it was occupied by other units.

Our chief losses, however, were through illness. Captain P. H. Creagh, whose splendid work was rewarded by a D.S.O., left us at the end of August for good, and joined his own regiment in Mesopotamia. Before the end of September, Captain C. H. Williamson, the Brigade's excellent Signalling Officer (afterwards killed in action); Captain A. H. Tinker, at that time Machine Gun Officer, but afterwards most admirable of Company Commanders; Captains H. H. Nidd and J. R. Creagh, most careful of Company Officers; D. Norbury of the Machine Guns; Pain and Pilgrim, invaluable Somerset officers attached to us, all left the Battalion with jaundice. Burn and Bryan left it with dysentery; Morten with a poisoned hand.

There was little indeed to cheer the men in the trenches. News percolated through to us of the failure at Suvla and of the hardships endured in that enterprise. Mails from home arrived all too slowly and precariously. Death was always present. We regretted the loss of Captain H. T. Cawley on the night of the 23rd September. He had given up a soft billet as A.D.C. to a Major

General in order to share the lot of his old regiment, a battalion of the Manchesters, and was killed in a mine crater near Border Barricade.

The spell in the trenches admitted of few variations. The journey to them was always burdensome. It is easy to recall the trek, on the 1st October 1915, of weary, dust-stained, overloaded men some three miles up the nullah, inches deep in dirty dust and under a broiling sun, to occupy narrow fire trenches, unprotected as ever by head cover, and pestilential with smells and flies. Yet once established in the trenches, life was tolerable enough. As a Field Officer I was fortunate to be able to escape at times to enjoy the intense luxury of sea-bathing. Sometimes the evenings were misty, and the fog-horns of our destroyers and trawlers carried faintly across the Ægean Sea. More often the sunsets were gorgeous. The day always seemed long. Firing was frequent but targets were rare. Some men curled themselves up between the narrow red walls of the trenches, read, dozed, smoked, talked, one or two in each traverse observing in turns through the periscope across the arid belt of No Man's Land, where groups of grey-clad Turks, killed long ago, still lay bleaching and reeking under the torrid sky. Others foraged behind for fuel, which could only be found with great difficulty. A little later dozens of fires would be crackling in the trenches, with dixies upon them full of stew or tea. Flies hovered in myriads over jam-pots. The sky was cloudless. Heat brooded over all. No one ever visited the trench except the Battalion Headquarters Staff and fatigue parties with water-bottles. Many soldiers stripped to the waist, and wore simply their sun helmets and shorts. Sickness alone drew men away. The soil was dark red, caked and crumbling. Here and there the dead were buried into the parados, with such inscriptions as "Sacred to the Memory of an Unknown Comrade. *R.I.P.*"

The Mule Sap connected the trenches with Headquarters. We gathered curios, Turkish and German, from among its débris. At Headquarters the telephone, orderly-room and dressing-station alone denoted the presence of war. They were fixed in a beautiful ravine, looking upon a smooth sea, warm in the sunlight, with Imbros ten miles across the water. The meals were of first importance, but sandbags are uncomfortable seats, and the heat was trying. Pleasant it was in the cool of the evening to go to sleep with one's Burberry as a pillow. The stars shone kindly down, as they had shone long ago upon the heroes of the Iliad on the Plains of Troy, seven miles away across the Dardanelles, upon the Crusaders and Byzantines. You were asleep in a moment, and hardly stirred until 5 A.M., when it was time for "Stand to." Daylight moved quickly across the desolate waste, and by six o'clock another day of war and waiting had dawned.

The Territorial's thoughts turn to home far more often than do those of the Regular, for to him the family has always been more important than the regiment. H. C. Franklin, who took P. H. Creagh's place as our Adjutant at the end of August, and was an old Regular soldier of the Manchester Regiment, often said that the week's mail of a Territorial battalion is as large as six months' mails for a unit of the old Army. He told, too, a good story, which shows the perceptiveness of Indians. He was standing near to some Indian muleteers when the Manchester Territorial Brigade disembarked on Gallipoli. He heard them say in Hindustani : " Here is another of the regiments of shopkeepers." One pointed to Captain P. H. Creagh, our Adjutant and only Regular officer. He said : " But he is a soldier." Another said of Staveacre : " A fine, big man, but he also is of the shopkeepers."

The story of trench warfare during these months on Gallipoli is undramatic. A record of their little episodes is almost trivial. Yet this want of movement and initiative is true to life, and was the common lot of the three or four British Divisions then responsible for operations at Cape Helles. The campaign, in fact, came to a standstill on the failure of the great offensive in August. The objects of the Army were simply to hold the ground so hardly won in the first two months of the expedition, and to contain as large as possible a Turkish force on Gallipoli for the benefit of our Russian Allies in the Caucasus and elsewhere. The first of these objects was attained in spite of the thinness of our line, the universal inferiority of our positions to those of the enemy, and the gradual improvement of their guns and aircraft. The Nizam—*i.e.* the Regular first-line Turkish troops—had been practically destroyed. The remainder lacked the offensive spirit after their heavy losses in August, and perhaps their hearts were not sufficiently in the struggle to welcome further sacrifice of life, with time already running in their favour. We heard of one British officer who had acted as a hostage during a short armistice at Anzac. The Turks loaded him with presents of fruit, and, pointing to their dead on the battle-field, said : " So much for your diplomatists and diplomacy ! "

Our second object, also, is believed to have been gained, so far as was possible, having regard to our inadequate numbers and to the limitations of our technique of the period. Bombing used at this time to be practised by small sections in each battalion, who occupied dangerous salients called " bird-cages " in the fire trenches. Here in our Battalion, G. Ross-Bain and W. H. Barratt among the officers, S. Clough and T. Hulme among the N.C.O.'s—all valiant men—won a modest measure of fame. On one occasion Hulme picked up a live bomb thrown by the enemy and saved his comrades' lives by throwing it over the parapet with splendid self-devotion. Our British sappers became more proficient in mining, special corps being formed from among the Wigan colliers of the Manchesters and the Lowland Scots. The guns were always active, and their co-operation with the infantry was perfected. Those who remember passing by night along the winding length of Inniskilling Inch will recall the red lamp that marked the artillery forward observation officer's post at the corner of Burlington Street, and the well-hidden gun emplacement, where Greenheys Lane ran out of the Mule Sap. The familiar street signs carried men's minds back to Manchester.

CHAPTER VI

THE STRAIN

IN the second week of October, 1915, the Army at Cape Helles was reinforced by dismounted Yeomanry from East and West Kent, Surrey and Sussex, and by some Royal Fusilier Territorial units from Malta, who were lent to the Royal Naval Division. Many West Kent officers and N.C.O.'s were for a time attached to the Battalion, and proved admirable comrades. The 42nd Division received some scanty drafts on the 23rd October. These came from the 3rd line units at Codford on Salisbury Plain, and were of excellent quality. Our draft was under Lieutenant C. S. Wood, a very able signaller.

I noted on the 21st October that of the 300 men of the Battalion then in the field, nearly 100 were on detached jobs—signallers, machine gunners and details attached to various headquarters.

The result of the shrinkage in strength was a great strain upon the survivors. "We never sleep," the Battalion's motto, was adopted grudgingly as a rule of life. The necessities of the firing line required vigilance by day and night, and the long frontages allotted to the various units of the 42nd Division entailed broken nights

THE STRAIN

and laborious days for all. The men's physique became lowered. Septic sores were general; bad eyes, not infrequent; jaundice of a type indicating para-typhoid was common; amœbic dysentery very prevalent. Loss of health meant loss of vigour. Limited to one bottle of water a day for all purposes, and perpetually a prey to flies, heat, diarrhœa and want of rest, the soldier had a trying time. Rations of a type welcome in a northern climate were unpalatable in Turkey. In July and August we were liberally supplied with vegetables and raisins, and with much-prized golden syrup for our porridge; but the latter luxury then disappeared, while for several months our only vegetables were onions, which do not appeal to every palate. Jams, even when the pots were adorned with pictures of one Sir Joseph Paxton, had very diminishing attractions. The only strawberry jam we ever had on the Peninsula came to us in tins, from which the labels had been stripped by some kindly act of Providence. In the expedition's early days our men had been able to exchange English jams for dainties procurable by the French and Senegalese, but the monotonous and indefinable " plum and apple " of the later summer killed the trade and extinguished all foreign admiration of British jam-making. Only the flies were fascinated.

Our East Lancashire Territorials did all that was possible to relieve the strain. We had a most able medical officer in Captain J. J. Hummel, of Glasgow, who had temporarily succeeded

Captain J. F. Farrow (our own veteran M.O.) in July, but indeed all the units were happy in their doctors, and *emetine* in dysentery cases was a gift of gold. Nor could a Brigade have had a more gallant and untiring padre than Captain E. T. Kerby. He and Captain Farrow both won the Military Cross. Kerby must have said the burial service over the graves of nearly a thousand Manchesters on Gallipoli.

The food difficulty we met by encouraging unofficial imports. The kindness of all at home was beyond praise. Consignments of comforts were well regulated by Major H. G. Davies, who had charge of the Manchester depot, but many came direct from innumerable friends and national and local organisations. One mother of two boys of the Battalion who had lost their lives wrote to me, while sending parcels for their surviving comrades : " I dare say that life is dreary for them, poor lads. God in His mercy has been so very merciful in that my Darlings have been spared so much. My prayers will follow you throughout, praying for the success of the whole of Our Battalion, and that you may all be spared to come safely home to the fond hearts waiting."

England need never despair while she has such mothers.

The great glory of the East Lancashire Division during the long-drawn days of October and November was, however, the temper of its men. The spiritual exaltation, that all races feel at the

THE STRAIN

outbreak of war and in the hour of battle, disappears under the pressure of the daily grind. Then, in his divine good-nature, the British Tommy comes into his own. Nothing dims his cheerfulness and humour. A chorus starting with: "We are the M.G." proclaimed the jollity of our Machine Gun Section and the ingenuity of Sergeant W. Harrison. A Machine Gun Corps of the larger type, organised under the energetic command of Captain Hayes, was a thing of the future. A long list of singers and performers—Hartnett, Mort, Addison (of ragtime celebrity), Wheelton, Holbrook, Hoyle, Clavering, Shields—adorned the programmes of our concerts. Other men like Tabbron and F. E. H. Barratt were notably cheery souls in the lines. The handful of surviving officers—Higham, Chadwick, Whitley, Douglas—with a few excellent attached officers—J. Baker and J. W. Barrett of the Somersets, and F. W. Woodward of the Sherwood Foresters—were untiring promoters of the men's well-being.

Their wants were so modest. Old magazines and football editions of Saturday evening papers, published a month or two earlier in England, sufficed for their literary appetites. Lancashire boys are not brought up to read; the *Sentry* writers were exceptional. When I once came upon a man reading the *Golden Treasury*, in Hardship Avenue, I knew he could not be a Manchester man. He was not. He came from the Isle of Man, and had joined our reserves at Southport. I found about half-a-dozen men who could enjoy *The Times* broadsheets. I am afraid *John Bull* was much more popular.

It was pleasant indeed to stroll along the narrow trenches and see how staunchly the men forgot their privations. Towards evening little parties would go, heavy-laden, into long forward saps that the engineers had thrown forward from Inniskilling Inch, to pass the night in cuttings called "T-heads," which were ultimately to be connected together and form a new trench closer to the enemy. They looked out from these lonely places in the midst of No Man's Land upon scattered heaps of corpses, and in their front upon the well-built Turkish trenches, substantially wired in and full of cleverly disguised loopholes. Two sentries were placed in each "T-head." The man on watch was exposed to oblique fire from all directions, as both British and Turkish lines curved to right and left, while the constant sound of Turkish picks at work suggested the proximity of mines. The sap that ran back to the fire trench was very narrow, and ended in a low tunnel under our parapet. It was therefore hard to bring wounded in from the "T-head." I remember one poor fellow in A Company called Renshaw being badly wounded in the head one night, and being dragged back through the tunnel with infinite difficulty.

The Turks were quick to pick up targets. One morning at our bivouac on Geoghegan's Bluff, we noticed half-a-dozen mules stray from Gully Ravine to the moor on the summit of its southerly side, perhaps a thousand yards from the enemy's front

THE STRAIN

line. We saw them shot, one by one, within a minute. As the Turks enjoyed the possession of higher ground everywhere from first to last, their power of observation was necessarily greater than ours, and no corner of Cape Helles was exempt from shell fire. It pursued us even in our bathing places.

The course of life on Gallipoli was, however, so monotonous that men became callous to all dangers. They carried on the long day's routine and the numberless little jobs included in the term " trench duties," as if nothing else mattered. Such tasks are familiar to-day to so many millions of Europeans that they need no description. Gas masks, sprinklers and gongs were ready for use in every trench, but were happily not needed.

Our men represented every Lancashire type, from the master builder to the barrister's clerk, from the wheelwright to the calico printer, from the railway carter to the commercial traveller. You would find together in one traverse Sergeant J. V. H. Hogan, a well-read ex-Socialist devotee of Union Chapel debates and old political opponent of my own, and another sergeant, whose name I cannot now recall, but who had been the petty officer of a South American liner sunk by the *Karlsruhe* in the early days of the War. Then we had famous footballers in Sergeants Pearson and Bamber. The Territorial origin of the Battalion was, indeed, a never-failing source of strength. Officers and men came from the same place, enjoyed the same interests and possessed the same outlook. It was pleasant to see in the trenches, faces familiar in my own suburb of Fallowfield, and to chat with hundreds of men whose lives had touched mine in days of peace.

The worth and capacity of these men were not peculiar to our unit, but were common to the Manchester Brigade and the whole Division. One battalion contained expert miners. Another battalion, at this time commanded by Major (afterwards Lieutenant-Colonel) C. L. Worthington, had lost enormously in their valiant battles. One of their captains—R. H. Bedford—helped in our history lectures. Another battalion, under Lieutenant-Colonel MacCarthy Morrogh, with Major H. C. F. Mandley as Second in Command and Captain E. Horsfall as Adjutant, were our constant neighbours and allies. With the Lancashire Fusiliers and East Lancashires, and with the admirably run A.S.C. and R.A.M.C. we enjoyed a slighter but no less hearty friendship.

The best relief from the long strain of the trenches was a bathe in the sea, but any diversion while in rear of the firing line was exhilarating. We used to gather on the moors that lay between Geoghegan's Bluff and Bruce's Ravine, Turkish cartridge boxes made by the Deutsche Waffen und Munitionsfabriken at Karlsruhe and labelled with inscriptions in German and Turkish, innumerable spent Turkish cartridges, abandoned Mäuser rifles, Turkish bandoliers (stamped with the English name "Warner's") and all the usual fascinating débris of battle.

C COMPANY, THE BRITISH CAMEL COMPANY, KHARTUM.

THE STRAIN

On the 19th October I made a special expedition, with Captain C. E. Higham, to the southern sector of the area, where the French had held the line ever since their move from Kum Kale to the Peninsula. We walked to beautiful Morto Bay, with its graceful curve from the headland called De Tott's Battery. The ruins on this point, carried by the South Wales Borderers on the 25th April, stood out clear-cut against the bright blue of the Dardanelles and the fainter grey of the Asiatic coast beyond. We went on past French and Senegalese dug-outs to Sedd-el-Bahr, a village and fort wrecked by our naval guns in the first days of the campaign. The country was open and dotted with the remains of vineyards. North of Sedd-el-Bahr was the well-tended French graveyard, more prettily kept than our own cemetery above Lancashire Landing. Here sleep many hundred soldiers, "morts sur le champs d'honneur," their *képis* on the crosses, and their graves adorned by flowers. The Jews and Senegalese had their own separate plots.

Sedd-el-Bahr appeared to be but a collection of outer walls and broken pillars, posts and fountains, some of archaic design. On the beach below, the *River Clyde* recalled the glory of the landing of the Dublins, Hampshires and Munsters. We struggled back to our bivouac in the teeth of a dusty, warm wind, to be inoculated with *emetine* and to rest by the white coast road, while we watched our monitors riding between Cape Helles and Imbros, and landing shells in the Turkish trenches on the slopes of Achi Baba. On such an occasion Ross Bain would arrive from marketing among the Greeks on Tenedos with some greatly valued potatoes, and then all our troubles would be forgotten.

When rain came, the joy of living was hard to attain. During all our time on Gallipoli I remember but one or two occasions when we were fortunate enough to secure timber or some corrugated iron to roof our dug-outs. Normally we had only our mackintosh sheets. Rain turned the thick dust to a brown morass, and the little mule carts struggling past the swampy curve of Geoghegan's Bluff could hardly clamber up the Gully Ravine. It was choked with mud.

Then the sun would come out and the flies returned in their myriads to plague us. They blackened every jam-pot and clustered thickly round the mouths and eyes of sleeping soldiers. The trenches became dry and dusty. Detached legs or feet or arms of the dead would protrude from the parapet, as the soil around them fell away. Smells became all-pervading. We would seek refuge in the dug-outs, that looked out upon a crowded graveyard from the sloping incline by Border Barricade. Then would come the time for another inoculation with *emetine*, and we would join the long line of men waiting, stripped to the waist, for Captain Hummel's needle. We prayed that it might be effective, and that we should be spared the curse of dysentery and long nights of misery in and about the fly-infested latrines.

Military Cross. He became Staff Captain at Ismailia. W. F. Creery joined the Connaught Rangers and was mentioned in dispatches.

Another hero of the men's reminiscences was Captain A. H. Tinker. One night during the first month of the campaign a working party had lost itself on the moor. It was so dark that they ran great risk of straying into the enemy's lines—a fate that befell a number of our men at this period in that broken country. In spite of the proximity of the Turks, Tinker left the trenches and boldly sought the men himself, calling out loudly for them. They heard him and made their way back.

The days of initiative and enterprise had, however, passed. The wind and grit gave the strongest of us sore throats and high temperatures, and I gradually joined the crowded ranks of sick men "on light duty only." At the beginning of November we moved to the northern extremity of the Allies' line across the Peninsula, and here I saw the last phase of our warfare on Gallipoli. Sir Ian Hamilton had gone. All ideas of a renewed offensive had disappeared. After the 24th October the Turks enjoyed direct communication with Germany, and at Cape Helles there was no sign of revived strategy or rejuvenated tactics. Our work was simply to carry on and hold out. Some of the other Divisions took steps to guard their men against the menace of a "Crimean winter" by preparing sheltered quarters. Great flights of geese used to fly in V-shaped formations high over our heads on their way from Russia to

THE LIMIT

Egypt. They were augurs of our own eventual migration.

The new position of the Battalion was on Fusilier Bluff, a mile to the west of the ruins of Krithia. The left ran straight down to the sea, where monitors used to shell the enemy's positions, while destroyers watched the flank, and at night played flashlights on the ravine that divided us from the next bluff, where the Turks were entrenched. This ground had been won in the brilliant British advance of the 28th June. The Turkish line was close to ours, and our men were always on the strain. Incidents were common. On the 2nd November a Turk crawled along the beach with a white flag, and surrendered. At night the Turks built up in front of their parapet, and two were shot by Sergeant Stanton. One of our men was killed and two were wounded. On the 3rd, another man was killed by a bomb, while the daily drain of sickness went on unabated. General Elliott, at this period our Brigadier, was an energetic pioneer of new methods and more vigorous tactics. He had the Mule Saps improved.

Even, however, in the secluded Headquarters at Bruce's Ravine I could not keep my health, and Hummel's art was unavailing.

The average soldier on Gallipoli broke down after a month or two. Comparatively few endured more than three months. Of our officers only Scott (the Quartermaster) and Fawcus were on the Peninsula from start to finish, though

Colonel Canning, Higham and Chadwick had almost as fine a record. Few of the sick came back to Turkey.

Some, like my first batman Dinsdale, died in hospital at Alexandria or in Malta. Many went to England and passed into other units. Others rejoined later in Egypt. Somehow, in peace times we had never imagined that the Battalion could be so dispersed and broken.

My departure from Gallipoli is perhaps worth a description. Would that the wounded heroes of the landing could have received a hundredth part of the same care!

I left Border Ravine at six in the evening of the 5th November 1915, with a high temperature, and feeling very ill. I walked down to the 1st Field Ambulance Dressing Station in "Y" Ravine, where Captain Fitzgerald, R.A.M.C., directed me on to the base of that Ambulance in Gully Ravine. Here my servant, Hawkins, left me, and two medical orderlies carried my traps. Alas, I left behind me a much-prized Turkish copper basin and bayonet, spoils of war, which I never saw again. We walked two miles along the rough and dusky beach, a full tide washing over our feet and throwing many dead mules high upon the pebbles. At the station I got a cup of hot milk, and spent the night on a stretcher. Next morning my case was diagnosed as one of fever and swollen glands, by Captain John Morley, R.A.M.C., most brilliant of surgeons, and at ten o'clock (cherishing a label marked "Base") I

THE LIMIT 69

was swirled off in a motor ambulance to No. 17 Stationary Hospital above the beach known as Lancashire Landing since its glorious capture by the Lancashire Fusiliers on the 25th April. At 4.15 in the afternoon we motored off once more and boarded a steam launch, whence we transshipped to an uncomfortable lighter. At 6.30, in the dark, we were lifted by a crane into the P. & O. hospital ship *Delta*, where 500 sick and wounded were being collected. Dinner consisted of bread and milk only for many of us, but we revelled in the luxury of bed and bath. Next morning I sat on the sunny side of the deck. The shady side, chilly in the November air, looked out upon Cape Helles, with Achi Baba rising straight behind it, and to the left upon the grey succession of landing-places, enshrined in so many English hearts.

We sailed the next morning, and thus avoided the misery of the great November blizzard on the Peninsula.

The Division remained on the Peninsula until the 29th December. Dysentery abated and the flies vanished, but gale and storm carried on the strain, and frostbite was added to the men's trials. The Turks seem to have much increased their supply of munitions, and the loss of life continued day by day. "Asiatic Annie" and other guns across the straits showed renewed activity. A mine explosion on the 4th December killed one of our men and injured eight. Two popular privates, Hancock and Lee, were killed on Christmas Day. One singular innovation was the Turkish practice of shooting steel-headed darts from their aeroplanes. Their chance of striking any man was, luckily, very small.

Nothing daunted the spirit of East Lancashire. Our men held concerts to the very last, and the football eleven survived three rounds of an Army Corps competition, losing their tie in the fourth round on a field in which shells burst repeatedly to the discomfort of the players. Captains J. F. Farrow, F. Hayes and E. Townson returned to strengthen the small band of officers, while R. J. R. Baker, who had been intercepted on his way out and sent to Suvla Bay, was released for service with us.

It is easy to criticise in the light of a later standard. Gallipoli was invaded early in 1915, not in 1916 or 1917, when the whole technique of assault had been revolutionised. We landed with the methods practised in England since the Boer War, methods as out of date in France in 1917 as Wellington's methods were in 1915. On later knowledge no one can doubt that a vast concentration of gun power, infinitely equipped and munitioned, a scientific use of barrage fire, nicely adjusted to the movements of a great infantry force, itself organised to develop the fullest use of machine guns, Lewis guns, and grenades, would have broken the defences of Achi Baba. Our Army knew none of these advantages. The artillery was inadequate and was inadequately supplied with high explosives to prepare for an attack in the style afterwards perfected on the Western Front. It was realised nowhere at this period that the rôle of infantry in attack is quite secondary to that of the guns. The bombardment that preceded the infantry assaults at Cape Helles in August did not last over two hours, and certainly never hit the trenches actually in front of the Manchester Territorial Brigade. The gunners could do no more than they did. The resources at their disposal were quite insufficient to atone for the Army's difficulties in point of numbers and in point of ground. It would appear as if we enjoyed no real ascendancy over the enemy either in aircraft or mining. Bombing was most unfamiliar to us on arrival.

It appeals to the English sportsman greatly and came to be brilliantly practised, but it was rarely a determining element. The Battalion bombers on Gallipoli were officially known as Grenadiers. Steel hats were, of course, unknown. They would have saved many lives. Visual signalling, on which pains had been lavished during training, proved of little use. The telephone, however, was a godsend, and in our Battalion was admirably worked by Sergeant Stanton.

The one handicap that was above all others a constant and pervading thought in the minds of our men was the shortage in numbers. It was a common belief that more reinforcements would have carried the great advances of June and July over every obstacle. Our drafts were always too small and too few, and the want of men infinitely aggravated the exhaustion of the survivors. With but a part of its old strength, and with no supports whatever between itself and the beaches, a battalion was still expected to hold the same length of line as when it was up to strength. Some two hundred men, for instance, occupied the long stretch of trenches from Skinner's Lane corner to the eastern bird-cage and its numerous forward saps, upon which men had once been employed. The task involved weeks of scanty and broken sleep, and caused our support and reserve lines to be utterly untenanted. Fatigue work was necessary the very hour that a unit had straggled down to a bivouac from the fire trenches. So precious was man power that the doctors were forced to keep unfit men at duty until they dropped. It is impossible to imagine men more worn by sleeplessness and sickness than the jaded Manchester Territorials at the end of a fortnight in the front line. On a moving day Gully Ravine was littered with men who had fallen out of the ranks of a dozen regiments as they trudged, heavily laden, along the winding and dust-swept track.

Sir Ian Hamilton wrote of our men early in August: "The Manchesters are a really good Battalion. Indeed, the whole of that Brigade have proved themselves equal to veteran Regulars. The great misfortune has been that there are no drafts ready to fill them up quickly. Had they been at once filled up, as is the case in France, they would be finer than ever. As it is, I fear lest the remnants may form too narrow a basis for proper reconstruction when ultimately the drafts do make their appearance."

The drafts we received on Gallipoli were the cream of the 2nd and 3rd reserve lines, which had been organised at home under Colonels Pollitt and Hawkins. They gave up their ease and often their ranks in order to serve England better, but their numbers were small. The work of reconstruction, to which Sir Ian Hamilton looked forward, came afterwards in Egypt.

Sometimes the infantryman wondered whether, even if the essential reinforcements arrived, they would ensure victory. On this point it is difficult to judge. The home Government had committed itself to the project of an offensive on the Western

Front in the autumn of 1915, in spite of the huge obstacles that confronted the Allies in that theatre of war. The tactics of the period did not even organise trench raids.

The memory that dominates all recollections of Gallipoli is that of the grandeur of the British soldier. Though he took no part in the miracle of the landings, the East Lancashire Territorial proved himself worthy of comradeship with even "the incomparable 29th Division." He ranked with the Anzac and the Lowland Scot in the great adventure. The original 1st-line of our Battalion were really destroyed in Turkey with their comrades of the same Brigade, but their gallantry in the early assaults and their inflexible fortitude in the trenches—pestered by flies, enfeebled by dysentery, stinted of water, and worn out by hardships—are a lasting title to honour.

Their story, as told in the pages of the *Sentry*, was read by General Wingate a few months later " with mixed feelings of joy and sorrow—sorrow for the many good friends who have laid down their lives for their King and Country, and joy that it has fallen to the lot of the gallant Battalion, of which I have the honour to be Colonel, to have behaved so gloriously in one of the hardest and most deadly campaigns in which British troops have ever been engaged."

It is a source of pride to have known and lived with such men.

CHAPTER IX

REVIVAL IN EGYPT

A LARGE proportion of the sick and wounded invalided from Gallipoli became familiar with one or other of the Alexandria hospitals. I spent a week at Victoria College, which had become No. 17 General Hospital, with Sister Neville, whose devotion to duty the Battalion had learnt when at Khartum, as Matron. Thence I went to No. 10 Convalescent Hospital at Ibrahimieh, once the stately house of an interned German called Lindemann but now converted into a comfortable home under the care of Mr and Mrs Scott. British leniency still reserved its tempting orangery for the use of local Huns. It is the English way.

When the evacuation of Gallipoli was contemplated, every hospital was cleared as far as possible of inmates, and I was one of the many officers who in early December were turned adrift either to the hotels of Alexandria or the great waiting camps of Mustapha and Sidi Bish.

The mere narrative of a holiday period at Alexandria has no public interest. We learnt to know Levantine and Egyptian mentality better than ever. When at Khartum an Egyptian *dobey* (washerman) had amused us by soliciting Regimental custom in preference to his competitors, not on the ground that he washed clothes better or charged less, but solely, he said, because the other *dobeys* were "terribly wicked men." So at Alexandria, every pedlar was the one honest follower of his craft. Yet its population is more European than Egyptian. The shops were full of the picture post cards of Italy and France, and portraits of Venezelos were to be seen everywhere, adorned with the pale blue and white national colours of Greece. Probably Mr Lloyd George's fame enjoys even wider bounds. I have seen his likeness enshrined in wattle huts at Omdurman and Wadi Halfa.

I touched unfamiliar minor issues of the War on the two occasions when I sat as a member of the military court, which sits for the purpose of enforcing proclamations issued by the supreme British military authority in Egypt, and thus tides over the time that has to pass before the Capitulations are abolished and a regular system of uniform justice established. A day thus spent at the Carracol Attarine gives a fine insight into the blessings of British occupation.

Most of the cases that I heard turned on the adulteration and falsification of liquors. Egypt has had no licensing laws; and no effort to apply elementary principles of fair dealing to the drink trade had apparently been made until initiated under military law for the protection of the troops. Foreign wine dealers at Alexandria consequently flooded the market with spurious liquor, concocted from the weirdest raw materials. The only genuine claim they could set up for their merchandise was that it was at all events alcoholic. Owing to the utilisation of refuse beet and potatoes, alcohol is cheap in Egypt. By blending pure alcohol to the extent of anything up to ninety per cent. of the whole concoction with any particular paste or colouring matter, it is open to wine dealers to pass off any liquid as the most popular of wines or spirits. Case after case came before the court, of beer made of alcohol and powder; wine of colouring matter, alcohol and paste; brandy of "essences"; and bitters of "Chinese elixirs." The falsifying appliances came from Europe, but the bogus labels, which described those poisons as "specially adapted for invalids and bottled in Glasgow, Scotland," or even offered 25,000 francs to any who could prove that so-called Greek "Koniak" was not "the pure juice of the grape," were amusingly Levantine. British justice is sweeping away these pitfalls for the soldier and sailor.

Egypt was at this time a centre of Anzac relaxation. To have explored the tombs of the kings with a New Zealander, paced the roof of the Cairo Citadel with Australians, and watched the colonial celebrations of Christmas in the Alexandria streets is a political education. No Englishman after the War will be ignorant of that golden New World, where all the labour is well paid, all hours of work are limited, and all shops close at noon on Saturdays. In any competition for the glory of being God's own country

> "Australia will be there."

We were, however, at war. As a field officer, I had the duty of attending the burial of British soldiers in the Christian cemetery at Alexandria on Christmas Eve, 1915. Since the outbreak of the War the graveyard had extended from its original site, prettily shaded by foliage, over an adjacent waste of sand and rubble, where over 2500 of our men who died of wounds or disease at this base had already at this date been laid to rest. Here sleep many Manchester Territorials. In the midst of many graves, identified only by numbers, a black cross recalls the memory of Mundy, one of our gallant Company Sergeant-Majors.

On the 30th December 1915 I left Alexandria for the Dardanelles on the *Arcadian*, Sir Ian Hamilton's old ship, once most luxurious of steam yachts but destined to be torpedoed on the 15th April 1917 in these same waters. It carried some details for the various Divisions still believed to be holding Cape Helles. We sailed in long zigzags through a rough sea to within a few hours' distance from Lemnos. We were then ordered back by wireless to Alexandria, landing there, much to our chagrin, on the 6th January 1916. Two days later Cape Helles was evacuated. It was never known whether our departure from Egypt had been a piece of bluff designed to cloak the impending move from Gallipoli, or a sheer accident arising from ignorance at Alexandria of the true intentions of the Mediterranean Expeditionary Force Headquarters.

From the date of the *Arcadian's* return down to the end of January, the large waiting drafts at Alexandria remained in tantalising inactivity, in spite of the passage of the Gallipoli survivors southward through Alexandria. The East Lancashire details forgathered at Mustapha on the site of the famous victory of 1801, and near the pretty white obelisk that commemorates Sir Ralph Abercromby. The time was filled as best could be by route marches, history lectures and various competitions, until at last we had orders to rejoin the Division. We moved from Sidi Gaber station to Cairo, and thence by trams to Mena, where, with " forty centuries " looking down upon us, we found what was left of the Manchester Territorial Brigade, then under General Elliott's command. The Battalion numbered close on 300 men.

Our stay at Mena was short, for infinite labour was now urgently needed on the Sinai Peninsula. In the early stages of the War, the Suez Canal had been treated as itself the main obstacle to an attack on Egypt. Outlying posts like El Arish had been abandoned, and Sinai left almost bare of defences. This policy accounts for the ease with which the Turks had actually gained the Canal bank in February, 1915. It was now recognised that defensive lines should run on the Asiatic side of the Canal in order to make it impossible for any invader to come within gunshot of the waterway. Three possible routes were open to the enemy. The northerly coast road by El Arish and Katia was the best, and enjoyed a Napoleonic tradition, but naval co-operation made its defence easy. A central track ran from El Audjo at the end of the main Palestine railway embankment to Bir Hassana, and might be used against Ismailia. A southerly approach was possible through Akaba and Nekl, and thence by the main pilgrims' road, the Darb El Haj, to Suez.

The Division was now to be employed in creating some of the new posts of defence, by which all such dreams of attack were to be dispelled. The strategy was passive, but it paved the way for the offensive undertaken in the ensuing summer.

On the bitterly cold night of the 1st February 1916 we left Mena. Before noon on the 2nd they reached Shallufa sidings. In the evening they crossed the Canal, and bivouacked in gathering darkness on a desert site known later as Shallufa Camp. The days of rest were over.

CHAPTER X

ON THE SUEZ CANAL

DURING February of this year the Battalion was engaged upon an inner line of works within easy walking distance of the Canal. A semicircular outpost line, which covered these works and the Brigade camp, was occupied nightly, but there was no real danger of attack. Beyond the outpost line a distant screen of posts, whose names recalled Lancashire, were in course of construction.

Life under such conditions gave no scope for ideas. The men did set tasks as fatigue work. There was no tactical training. Gangs drew a chain ferry to and fro across the Canal, while Lieutenant A. N. Kay acted as wharfmaster. Several days were given to moving camp a few hundred yards north or south within a small area. Two detached posts were held at this period. One far out among the rolling sandhills, skilfully laid out by Captain A. H. Tinker, was known for a week or two as Ardwick, and then abandoned. Another, very ably commanded by Captain C. Norbury, was the far more fascinating blockhouse known as Gurkha Post, noted for its bathing, fishing and agreeable remoteness from staff officers. It was delightful to ride out from Shallufa camp along a track called " the pilgrims' way " to so charming a spot for a swim in the Canal and pleasures impossible on the dust-swept desert. A few hundred yards to the north, a little white tower called Lonesome Post long flaunted in red paint the Battalion's name and motto for the edification of passing liners. What have become of like devices that were once deep cut on the scarped cliff of Bruce's Ravine on Gallipoli ?

One amusing experience of this period was to bathe in the Canal while the transports were passing with newly trained drafts for Mesopotamia or India. " Who are you ? " was the invariable cry from the banks. Our war-worn men received usually the answering taunt : " Garrison duty only ! When are you going to do your bit ? " To the call : " Who are you ? " from a transport, a witty diver replied : " A submarine."

The whole Canal zone from Port Said to Suez was in reality a hive of workers. A visit to the School and Headquarters of the Royal Flying Corps threw a flood of light on that brilliant service. Its observers commanded every track and camping ground of the Sinai desert.

While the Canal was being girdled by defence works the Manchester Territorial Brigade was regaining the physical vitality lost in Turkey. Apart from sandstorms, the climate was good. Sports, football, concerts, buried-treasure hunts, competitions " for the singing championship of Asia " and other sounding honours, and much bathing helped us to recover health and joy. Our numbers remained much below strength. Perhaps 130 of the original unit remained, with some 250 who had come to Turkey in drafts. To these hardly 100 were added at this period.

Such officers and men, however, as did reach us from the two reserve units at home were of the best. They lost temporary rank on re-posting, and knew that weaker vessels had succeeded to their place on English camping grounds. Those who came from another battalion had been specially fortunate in their training, and in having the inspiring influence in their midst of Captain J. H. Thorpe, but all alike were keen. Their anxiety to learn was palpable whenever we went the round of the chilly desert outposts under the starry sky.

Battalion patriotism was kindled anew by the adoption as a flash of the old Lincoln green fleur-de-lis of the Manchesters, a cap badge worn by us since 1889, and a relic of the conquest of Guadaloupe by the 63rd Regiment in 1759. No less inspiring was the revival of the *Sentry* on the 1st March 1917. Of its staff of fifteen when published at Khartum, nine had died on Gallipoli. Their places were filled by new enthusiasts, and one genuine poet was discovered in T. G. King.

Our one lasting loss while at Shallufa was the departure of nearly all the time-expired Territorials to England. Those under forty-one years of age were retaken later by the Government under its new powers of conscription, but the Battalion

Back Row—Lieut. T. F. Brown, Lieut. N. H. P. Whitley, Lieut. J. H. Thorpe, Lieut. G. S. Lockwood.
Front Row—Capt. R. V. Rylands, Capt. H. Smedley.

ON THE SUEZ CANAL 85

saw few of them more. These men—W. Jones, Mort, Woods, Stanton, Fielding, Lyth, Bracken, Houghton, Dermody, Parkinson, Barber—were the salt of the Regiment. During the long years when Territorial service had been irksome and unfashionable, they made it succeed. With a few old hands like Regimental Quartermaster-Sergeant Ogden, who elected to remain with the unit, they had borne the burden of the trenches manfully, and never grumbled as to their status while commissions were showered on men at home whose claims, compared with theirs, were modest.

On the 24th March 1916 the Brigade left Shallufa, and on the morning of the 25th marched into Suez New Camp to undergo training. The move was welcome, as it was imagined to lead to a departure for a more active theatre of war.

The type of training adopted at Suez derived its inspiration from the French Army, whose text-books of 1916 taught that close order drill and punctilious discipline, tempered by games and sports, were ideal means of reviving the all-important offensive spirit in units.

The four and a half weeks spent by the Battalion at Suez were therefore crowded with field days and ceremonial drill. On the 21th May there was a striking review of the whole Division, followed by a march past in blinding dust. Days of this type, however, even if they mean rising at four in the morning and include Brigade bathes in the warm, blue Gulf of Suez, followed by breakfast on a sun-baked shore, are the same all the world over. They are not worth discussing in writing of the fateful time which witnessed the great German attack upon Verdun and Fort Douaumont.

At all events, Suez saw the reconstruction of the Manchester Territorial units completed. The sense of vitality, without which no army can take the offensive, was fully restored. We had spirited sham fights with another battalion of the Manchesters for the possession of " Tower 16," a solitary landmark on the caravan track to Cairo, after the manner of the pre-War era. The *Sentry* blossomed as the first English paper of the country. Two thousand copies used to be sold at Suez alone. Our men competed for Colonel Canning's football cup and played a great match with the crew of the *Ben-my-Chree*, the famous seaplane carrier, sunk by gunfire, alas, some eight months later in Kastelorizo Harbour. The "Flashes" gave notable concerts.

From the 21st April I again enjoyed the command of the Battalion. Colonel Canning went on leave to England, and his distinguished services were recognised soon afterwards by a C.M.G.

Towards the end of May, 1916, the Division was unexpectedly ordered to move from Suez, and broken up in order to supply battalions for digging work at various spots on the eastern side of the Canal—mainly on the then most advanced screen of detached infantry posts—where the existing defence scheme had not progressed with sufficient speed. A more combative strategy was

ON THE SUEZ CANAL

obviously contemplated, no doubt provoked by the recent action at Katia. In the late afternoon of the 25th May the Battalion started on their march into the Sinai Peninsula. The transport was left at Suez under Lieutenant M. Norbury and Sergeant A. B. Wells, and with Captain A. T. Ward Jones as Brigade Transport Officer.

Among the posts thrown out into the Peninsula, none at that time was more desolate or remote than the sandy ridge called Ashton-in-Sinai, apparently in honour of Ashton-under-Lyne. It lies many miles to the east of the Little Bitter Lake. The trek to this spot by way of Kubri and Shallufa was an ordeal even for our seasoned troops in the blazing heat of an African summer. At 3 A.M. on the 27th May the Battalion set out from their chilly bivouac by the Y.M.C.A. hut at Shallufa along a road made by the Egyptian Labour Corps to a site called Railhead, about ten miles off, where we rested during the broiling day. At four in the afternoon we started on the worst lap of the trek, a final two hours' ascent across the softest and heaviest sand imaginable to the high rolling dunes of Ashton.

CHAPTER XI

SINAI

THE view at Ashton is superb. Looking back on Africa, we saw on the horizon the pale contour of the Gebel Ataki beyond the silvery line of the Bitter Lakes and the Canal. On its Asiatic side, the detached posts of Oldham, Railhead, and Salford, held by other battalions of the Manchesters, glittered under a torrid sky amid the great waste of desert. Facing our front, the wilderness stretched towards Palestine in endless undulation.

The sultry days spent by the Battalion at Ashton were, however, spoiled by excessive heat and repeated sandstorms. Double-lined tents were only supplied after much delay, and promised wooden dining huts only approached completion by the time we left.

This arid outpost of Empire was linked to civilisation by a camel trail to Railhead. Its garrison duties were performed by some Essex Territorials, commanded by Lieutenant-Colonel Jameson, afterwards killed before Gaza. Yeomanry passed by frequently, scouting far into the waste. The Manchesters were occupied exclusively in digging trenches and in laying

SINAI

entanglements in the deep soft sand, "according to plan" and on a scale sufficient to daunt any invader who could have surmounted the huge physical obstacles that already barred all approach to this spot from the Wadi Muksheib and the East.

The arms of Britain have by now made these particular defences of the Canal of most trifling importance. Her foot is in Palestine. Work done at Ashton may well be gradually obliterated. Yet a few words can be said of the men who lived and laboured here in June, 1916, in a temperature rising often to 120° F. in the shade and rarely falling under 100° F. at night. No digging was practicable between 7.30 A.M. and 4.30 P.M. The men rose before four in the morning for the day's work. Progress was necessarily slow, partly owing to constant silting, partly to the common weakness of the authorities for varying the sites and types of the trenches. Materials were often wanting. Nevertheless the Manchesters won unqualified praise. Their civil life had fitted many for the task of reveting trenches with hurdles. The defences of Ashton-in-Sinai were improved in a few weeks beyond recognition.

One incident that occurred here illustrates amusingly the contrast between the outlooks of the new soldier and the old. Our Manchester Territorials were distressed to find that thousands of yards of hurdles were being lined with the best tent cloth at 1s. 4d. a yard, instead of with cheap cotton at a quarter the price. I repeated their plaint to a Regular officer of the old school, expecting sympathetic indignation. "Magnificent," was his reply. "It shows the world in what spirit England goes to war."

It was at Ashton that we first heard the news of the Jutland Battle from Colonel Fremantle, R.A.M.C., who could only give us the version spread by German wireless. A few days later we learnt of Lord Kitchener's death.

It is clear that this particular phase of soldiering has in itself no place in the annals of the Great War. Ashton is already nothing but a desert site. The tide of victorious warfare has left it high and dry. It always was high and dry. At probably no other period, however, did the personality of the Manchester Territorial show to greater advantage, as the life was one of peculiar privation. Water was carried up daily by camels from Railhead, but was most scanty, and always warm. The sand was too soft for any game to be played—too soft even to permit of trotting horses. The heat was constant and intense. The men were as cheerful and uncomplaining as ever.

To have developed such a spirit in men entirely civilian in habits and traditions was the glory of the Territorial system.

All ranks toiled together to make life in this corner of Sinai liveable. History hardly looks beyond the Army Corps at the smaller unit. Still less does she concern herself with the humble pawn in some unimportant corner of the great game. In reality, however, his lot is of moment

SINAI

to the race. The tone of an army is the tone of its individual men. An unhappy soldiery cannot win wars. "An army moves on its stomach," said Napoleon; and the recognition of the soldier's hunger and thirst, his desire for rest, amusement and sympathy helps, almost as much as skill and self-confidence help, to make the successful leader of men.

It was, therefore, a soldier's job to keep up the hearts of our colony at Ashton-in-Sinai. Captain C. Norbury, as acting President of Regimental Institutes, and Captain H. Smedley, as stage-manager and singer, worked on the only sound lines.

Journalism, theatrical performances, lecture courses, concerts and canteen business, as initiated and practised by the officers and men of the Battalion at Ashton, were true factors towards efficiency and discipline.

After three hours' work and their breakfast, the men would gather in our recreation tent with its flaps rolled up, and listen to a lecture on some historical or military subject which bore upon the topic of the hour. They then slept and smoked and played cards or sang through the long midday heat until the time came again for digging. In the evening, on a stage cleverly made by Sergeant Taylor, the dramatic company would act some play that appealed to their emotions, or a concert party would indulge them with a medley of ragtime and sentimental songs. Addison's *Stammering Sam* alternating with Sergeant

Shields' *When Irish Eyes are Smiling*. The taste of Lancashire is catholic.

On Sundays we often merged " Church and Chapel " in a common service. Davey, the Methodist padre, was an ex-gunner of the Royal Navy and a great athlete—attributes that enhanced his influence as preacher. " Crime," however, did not exist at Ashton-in-Sinai. Nor did temptations. The real danger was mental and physical deterioration under the depressing influence of the country and the climate, for the intense heat sapped every man's vitality. We set ourselves to combat these risks, and to give the men the food and recreation without which soldiering becomes a burden, and discipline degenerates to servitude.

Towards evening I would ride into the desert and watch from the east our men labouring on the great sand ridge in a haze of heat. On this side of Ashton there were no tracks at all. The eye could see nothing but endless sand hills, broken only by patches of dry scrub and shimmering yellow under the burning sun. If nature has changed little in the desert since Israel came out of captivity, it is easy to sympathise with their regret for the fleshpots of Egypt. So penetrating was the sun that the colour of the men's khaki breeches faded into purple.

There was, indeed, a certain charm in our remoteness from the outer world. Camping out in the wilderness had more than a touch of the desert island of boyish imagination. There was

SINAI

glamour in the extraordinary simplicity of a life where the higher command was but a distant name, and where men dressed themselves and spent the long, hot day as they pleased. The fret and competition of Europe were felt no more. I remember our arguing about Irish Home Rule one night till the stars paled in the eastern sky, but the episode was unique. In spite of its hardships, no manner of life was ever more calculated to banish ancient feuds, to strip human nature of envy and uncharitableness, or to mould that most perfect of all democracies—a brotherhood in arms.

On the afternoon of the 22nd June 1916 we left the wilderness under orders for Kantara. We spent several days near Shallufa sidings, and then, having obtained leave for England, I left for Suez with W. H. Barratt and W. T. Thorp, two subalterns who had made their mark while in the ranks by distinguished service in the field. Early in July we sailed from Port Tewfik to Marseilles and watched from its deck the distant camp of the Turkish prisoners from Arabia twinkling in the sunlight across the most southerly reaches of the Canal.

I need say no word more in praise of the men of our Battalion, whom I saw for the last time in my eighteen years of service resting in a dusty gorge near Shallufa. Knit together by common ideals and experiences, they were, in Nelson's phrase, " a band of brothers."

We crossed France from Marseilles to Boulogne

in an atmosphere of war. We had glimpses of Lyons and Paris, talked with *poilus* on leave, heard from a French officer (who professed to know) that the War would be over in March, 1917, and bought from vivacious street hawkers pretty metal souvenirs of Verdun. We saw our own wounded coming back in Red Cross trains from the first days of the great push on the Somme. Then, after exactly a year's absence, I was once more at home.

Within the ensuing month all but three of the original combatant officers still on the strength of the Battalion were seconded for service elsewhere. "The old order changeth, giving place to new." . . . .

A Regiment in war rises like the phœnix from its own ashes and renews its immortal youth. The vicissitudes here recorded fill but a few shining chapters in what will no doubt prove a long history. They by no means necessarily contain its most distinguished pages. The close of the second year of the Battalion's active service is, however, a fitting point to end this volume. It marked the stage at which the distinctively " 1st line " unit, composed of officers and men enlisted and trained voluntarily in time of peace, had passed into the normal type of British Battalion of 1916—a unit born of the War, with its personnel mainly recruited and trained after its outbreak.

It is to the memory of the original volunteers of August, 1914, that this book is dedicated.

CHAPTER XII

THE TERRITORIAL IDEA

THE experiences of a typical unit of the Territorial Force must throw light on the vexed questions that have gathered round it.

Three criticisms of the Territorial system have been made ever since its adoption in 1907. First, its establishment of 310,000 men has been regarded as totally inadequate, and before the War the country even failed to recruit numbers within sixty thousand of this modest standard. Secondly, its yearly training, which provided but a fortnight's life in camp, has been deemed so paltry as to be almost negligible. Thirdly, the Territorial and Reserve Forces Act 1907 provided a legal loophole by which the less patriotic could evade service overseas in however great an emergency. Section 13 specifically lays down that, apart from purely spontaneous offers by officers or men to serve abroad, " no part of the Territorial Force shall be carried or ordered to go out of the United Kingdom."

In reality, none of the defects which attracted these criticisms was inherent in the Territorial idea. They rather belonged to the whole military policy of the country before the War. Public opinion held that a European War was practically impossible, and that the British Army must of necessity be small in numbers and voluntary in character.

On these assumptions the limitations of the Territorial Force were simply inevitable. Having regard to the prevailing views on national defence and to the general resistance to Lord Roberts' propaganda, the Territorial scheme reduced the evils of voluntaryism to the minimum.

The difficulty as to its shortage in men was met as soon as War was declared. The Territorial Force was, in fact, capable of infinite expansion, and of being the basis of the entire New Army, had the Government so willed. Its training, again, was far better than no training at all. Later events have proved with what speed wholly untrained British conscripts can be moulded into efficient soldiers, and that willing men can learn discipline and the use of the rifle within a very few months. Territorial training sufficed, at any rate, to enable Territorial units to relieve the Regular Army of all garrison duties abroad immediately on the outbreak of war, and in many cases themselves to take the field on active service before Christmas, 1914. Even with regard to the constitutional obstacle to using the Force overseas, fully nine-tenths of its men never dreamed of claiming immunity. The small margin, which were left for employment in home defence, mainly represented the physically unfit or boys under age.

THE TERRITORIAL IDEA 97

As events turned out, two unexpected disadvantages of the system were generally experienced. In times of peace the Territorial Force had been able to influence public policy through the County Associations and the House of Commons. After embodiment, the Force itself became necessarily inarticulate under the conditions that govern all military service. Far less influential than the Regulars and far less numerous than the New Army, it went abroad early in the War, and was thus not actively in touch with Parliament, while the semi-civilian County Associations, whose personal and local knowledge might have been invaluable, ceased to have any powers over its organisation, and had no means of safeguarding its interests on questions of promotion, appointments, commands and pay.

An even more serious flaw arose from the dispersion of the Territorials all over the world from Gibraltar to Burmah in the first months of the War. An enormous volume of skilled labour was thereby lost to the country, and exemption from service, which might well have kept these men at home in the national interest, fell later to the lot of many younger and less expert workers in their stead. Moreover, a great number of men ideally fitted for commissions were killed fighting in the ranks or were allowed to serve obscurely in remote corners of the globe. Both among Territorial officers and men, a large proportion were qualified, by gifts of leadership, technical knowledge or familiarity with foreign languages, for special employment in Western Europe. There was indeed a demobilisation in this respect of a considerable proportion of the country's brain power.

Happily, the East Lancashire Territorials found an outlet for their qualities on Gallipoli.

Against all the defects that have no doubt affected the application of the Territorial idea, the historian should set its signal virtues. It is an asset beyond price in soldiering to have all ranks welded together by community of feeling and opinion. Joined by ties of neighbourhood, occupation, sport and common interests, men are particularly apt to cultivate that intense patriotism of the small unit which is termed *esprit de corps*. The history of the War—like the history of all past wars—will illustrate its constant military value. It would be idiotic to reassert the old fallacy, belied by the experience of centuries, that one volunteer is worth ten pressed men. Nevertheless the morale of a unit can only be enriched when it is recruited wholly from willing applicants familiar with its traditions and with the badges that symbolise its past, rather than from conscripts drafted from anywhere in Great Britain by the chance action of a Government department. Indeed the Territorial idea has counted for much wherever British man power has been successfully organised during the War.

Those who have believed in the Territorial Force during its struggles against popular apathy and professional distrust have been justified by its deeds in the field.

The true greatness, however, of the simple and unambitious Territorial soldiers, whose life and work are described in these pages, lies more in their spirit than in any actual achievements. All of them came from the industrial North, where the business of life is fiercely competitive, and where each man is wont to seek his own fortune without much outward consideration for his fellows. Yet in the field it would be impossible to imagine minds less touched by selfishness or less influenced by any notion of personal distinction or reward. They did their best for Britain. Honours are but gifts of the capricious gods.

Thus "to put the cause above renown" is a principle of conduct often identified with what is called the Public School spirit. Fortunately the temper which it expresses extends far beyond the governing class in England, and it animated the typical Territorial of the Great War. Like all good soldiers, he was far too inarticulate and reserved to think of putting it into words. His deeds spoke for him. *The Whitewash on the Wall* and *Hold your Hand out, Naughty Boy* are not beautiful songs, but the lads who have sung them in English lanes and Turkish gullies could have shown no greater self-devotion had their songs been as solemn as the Russian National Hymn, or as thrilling as the *Marseillaise*.

APPENDIX

The following is an extract from a letter on the work of the Battalion sent by General Sir F. R. Wingate, G.C.B., K.C.M.G., D.S.O., High Commissioner for Egypt, to the General-Officer-in-Chief of the Division, when the Battalion left the Sudan.

> GOVERNOR-GENERAL'S OFFICE,
> KHARTUM.
> 10*th April* 1915.

. . . during the few months they [the Battalion] have been in the Sudan they have become thoroughly efficient soldiers in the strictest sense of the term. Route marches, night operations, field days, hard drilling in the Barrack square, digging trenches, gun and maxim drill, and last but not least, constant practice on the ranges in addition to ordinary garrison duties have transformed them into an alert body of trained soldiers capable of taking their place anywhere. You can safely rely on them to do—and do well—whatever duty they may be called upon to perform against the enemy, and I am confident that they will yield to no Battalion in the Division in regard either to training or fighting efficiency. Should, by any chance, the Division be sent to

APPENDIX

the Near East, you will find in the Battalion upwards of one hundred men fully trained in camel riding and camel management, and this knowledge may prove useful under certain conditions, but of course I have no idea where the Division is to be sent and whether a knowledge of the numerous promiscuous duties required by Battalions garrisoning the Sudan will find an outlet.

A sound system of Interior Economy prevails in the Battalion, and the good organisation of the Regimental Institutes reflects much credit on all concerned with their management. During the time the Battalion has been in my Command the behaviour of all ranks has been exemplary—the men have made themselves liked by all in Khartum and are very popular with the natives.

I have the highest opinion of Colonel Gresham —he has an excellent lot of Officers, and both the Adjutant, Captain Creagh, and the Quarter-Master, Major Scott, have done particularly well. I am proud to be Honorary Colonel of such a fine Territorial Battalion.

We all are heartily sorry to bid them good-bye, and we wish them and the gallant Division which you Command every success and good luck wherever you may be.

Yours sincerely,
(*Signed*) R. WINGATE.

INDEX OF PERSONAL NAMES

(Italics signify that the person mentioned has been killed or has died of wounds)

Abercromby, Gen. Sir R., 80
Addison, J., 59, 91
Anderson, C., 42
Arnott, M., 27

Bacon, A. H., 40
Baker, J., 59
Baker, R. J. R., 70
Balfe, W., 27
Bamber, Sgt., 61
Barber, W., 85
Barratt, F. E. H., 59
Barratt, W. H., 54, 93
Barrett, J. W., 59
Basnett, J., 26
Bateman, M., 27
Beaumont, T., 7
Beckett, J., 42
Bedford, R. H., 62
Bedson, Capt., 27
Boyle, Major, 10
Bracken, W., 85
Bradbury, C. S., 42
Brown, J. N., 9
Brown, T. F., 24
Bryan, C. J., 50
Burn, F. G., 50

Canning, Lt.-Col. A., 28, 31, 37, 43, 68, 86
Cawley, H. T., 50
Chadwick, G., 35, 39, 40, 42, 59, 68
Cherry, W., 26, 42
Clavering, H., 46, 59
Clough, S., 54
Cookson, C., 27
Corris, J., 37
Creagh, J. R., 39, 40, 50
Creagh, P. H., 4, 26, 28, 31, 32, 37, 50, 53, 101
Creery, W. F., 65, 66

Darlington, Lt.-Col., 39
Davey, Lt.-Col., 92
Davidson, Judge, 17
Davidson, J., 88
Davies, H. G., 58
Dermody, W., 8
Dinsdale, T., 68
Douglas, C. B., 59
Dudley, C. L., 12, 26

Elliott, Brig. Gen. W., 67, 80
England, Lt.-Col. A., 48
Enver Pasha, 16

Farrow, J. F., 58, 70
Fawcus, A. E. F., 25, 31, 32, 36, 37, 42, 67
Fielding, W., 85
Fletcher, J., 42
Franklin, G. W. F., 37, 42
Franklin, H. C., 26, 53, 65
Freemantle, W. G., 25, 26
Fremantle, Lt.-Col. F. E. 90
George, D. Lloyd, 14
Gordon, Gen. G. C., 14
Granger, T. S., 27
Gresham, Lt.-Col. H. E., 3, 12, 23, 101

Haldane, Viscount, 3
Hamilton, A., 42
Hamilton, G. Hans, 8, 26
Hamilton, Gen. Sir Ian, 28, 33, 34, 66 79
Hancock, L., 69
Harrison, W., 42, 59
Hartnett, M., 48, 59
Hawkins, Lt.-Col. H., 74
Hawkins, I., 68
Hayes, F., 27, 59, 70
Hayes, Pte., 42
Heys, Lt.-Col., 27
Higham, C. E., 25, 59, 63, 68
Hogan, J. V. H., 61
Holbrook, J., 59
Horsfall, E., 62
Houghton, Pte., 85
Hoyle, H., 46, 59
Hulme, T., 42, 54
Hummel, J. J., 57, 64, 67

James, Capt., 27
Jones, J. C., 7
Jones, W., 85
Joyce, J., 42

Kay, A. N., 82
Kerby, E. T., 58
King, T. G., 84
Kitchener, Earl, 14, 71, 90

INDEX OF PERSONAL NAMES

Lawrence, Maj.-Gen. H. A., 34
Lee, Brig.-Gen. N., 5, 27
Lee, B., 69
Leigh, A., 42
Lindsay, W., 27
Lingard, J. R., 30
Lockwood, G. S., 23
Lyons, J. P., 20
Lyth, J., 85

MacCartney, H. L., 37
M'Hugh, S., 26, 42
Maher, T., 42
Mandley, H. C. F., 62
Marvin, W., 27, 65
Masefield, J., 33
Morley, J., 19, 68
Morrogh, Lt.-Col. M., 62
Mort, W., 40, 48, 59, 85
Morten, J. C., 50
Mundy, A., 27, 79
Murphy, Pte., 42

Nelson, D., 9
Neville, Sister M.,
Newbigging, Col. W. P. E., 2
Nidd, H. H., 50
Norbury, B., 12
Norbury, C., 12, 26, 82, 91
Norbury, D., 50
Norbury, G., 27
Norbury, M., 87

Ogden, T., 85

Pain, R., 50
Palmer, F. C., 25
Parkinson, W., 85
Pearson, Sgt., 61
Pilgrim, H., 50
Pilkington, Lt.-Col. C. R., 30
Pollitt, Col. J. B., 74
Powell, A., 6

Renshaw, C., 60
Richardson, Pte., 26
Roberts, Earl, 3, 96
Ross Bain, G., 54, 64
Rylands, R. V., 12, 24

Savatard, T. W., 10, 24
Scott, J., 4, 67, 101
Shields, J., 59, 92
Smedley, H., 36, 37, 42, 50, 91
Smyth, Col., 21
Stanton, J., 67, 85
Stanton, W., 73
Stuveacre, J. H., 3, 14, 20, 24, 26, 31, 50, 65
Sutherland, J. W., 26

Tabbron, W., 59
Taylor, J., 91
Thewlis, H. D., 25, 26
Thorp, W. T., 42, 93
Thorpe, J. H., 8, 12, 84
Tinker, A. H., 50, 66, 82
Towson, E., 9, 70

Venezelos, 77

Walsh, Pte., 42
Ward, Lt., 27
Ward Jones, A. T., 87
Webster, Sgt., 27
Wells, A. B., 87
Wheelton, S., 59
White, F., 40
Whitley, N. H. P., 8, 59, 65
Williamson, C. H., 50
Wilson, Col., 17, 20
Wingate, Gen. Sir F. R., 10, 13, 14, 21, 75, 101
Wingate, Lady, 14, 21
Wood, C. S., 56
Wood, J. W., 48, 85
Woodward, F. W., 59
Worthington, Lt.-Col. C. R., 62

www.ingramcontent.com/pod-product-compliance
Lightning Source LLC
LaVergne TN
LVHW091308080426
835510LV00007B/411